Studies in Christianity
and Judaism / Etudes sur le
christianisme et le judaïsme : 1

Studies in Christianity and Judaism /
Etudes sur le christianisme et le judaïsme

Studies in Christianity and Judaism / Etudes sur le christianisme et le judaïsme presents publications that study Judaism and Christianity together in an effort to reach an understanding of how the two religions have related and relate to each other as well as studies that offer original insight into some central aspect of the two religions or of one of them. Three groups of studies are envisaged: studies of doctrine, historical studies, and textual studies. Whereas there exist similar publications produced in Canada in a theological context, this Series reflects the specific nature and orientation of the departments of religious studies in Canadian centres of learning. In these departments Christianity and Judaism are studied from the perspective of the history of religions. Such a perspective is not necessarily aligned with one of the two traditions. It tries to transcend traditional antagonisms as well as confessional limitations. After several decades of work from such a perspective Canadian scholars are now in a position to offer studies that put forward less conventional views of the two religions.

A STUDY IN ANTI-GNOSTIC POLEMICS

Irenaeus, Hippolytus, and Epiphanius

Gérard Vallée

Studies in Christianity and Judaism /
Etudes sur le christianisme et le judaïsme: 1

Published for the Canadian Corporation for Studies in Religion / Corporation
Canadienne des Sciences Religieuses by Wilfrid Laurier University Press

Canadian Cataloguing in Publication Data

Vallée, Gérard, 1933-
    A study in anti-Gnostic polemics

(Studies in Christianity and Judaism = Etudes sur le
christianisme et le judaïsme, ISSN 0711-5903 ; 1)
Bibliography: p.
ISBN 0-919812-14-7

1. Irenaeus, Saint, Bishop of Lyons. Adversus haereses.
2. Hippolytus, Saint, fl. 217-235. Refutatio omnium
haeresium.   3. Epiphanius, Saint, Bishop of Constantia
in Cyprus.   Panarion.   4. Heresies and heretics—Early
church, ca. 30-600.   5. Gnosticism—Controversial
literature—History and criticism.   I. Title.
II. Series: Studies in Christianity and Judaism ; 1.

BT1390.V34   273'.2   C82-094052-6

81 82 83 84 85 4 3 2 1

Cover design by Michael Baldwin, MSIAD

Order from:
Wilfrid Laurier University Press
Wilfrid Laurier University
Waterloo, Ontario, Canada   N2L 3C5

TABLE OF CONTENTS

FOREWORD

In many ways this monograph is the result of a
corporate effort. It was prepared at McMaster University
under the auspices of a research project on Normative Self-
Definition in Judaism and Christianity funded by the Social
Sciences and Humanities Research Council of Canada. I am
thankful to SCM Press for permission to publish here as
chapter I a revised version of an essay that appeared first
in Jewish and Christian Self-Definition, Vol. I, The
Shaping of Christianity in the Second and Third Centuries
(ed. E.P. Sanders) 1980. Special thanks are due to
Professor Frederik Wisse (McGill University), who carefully
read my manuscript and made numerous stimulating comments
to which I have tried to live up; Professor Alan Mendelson
(McMaster University) and Dr. Tamar Frank, who contributed
editorial advice; Professor Pierre Nautin (École pratique
des Hautes Études, Paris), who allowed me to participate in
his seminar on Epiphanius in 1978-1979; and Professor
Norbert Brox (Universität Regensburg), whose writings and
friendly comments have inspired me throughout these years
of research. But, as usual, none beside myself should be
held responsible for the shortcomings of this work.

This book has been published with the help of a grant
from the Canadian Federation for the Humanities using funds
provided by the Social Science and Humanities Research
Council of Canada.

McMaster University
Hamilton
November 1980

ABBREVIATIONS

ACW	Ancient Christian Writers
Adv. haer.	Irenaeus, Adversus haereses (see chapter I, note 1)
Adv. Val.	Tertullian, Adversus Valentinianos
AHC	Annuarium historiae conciliorum. Amsterdam
ANF	The Ante-Nicene Fathers
BCNH	Bibliothèque copte de Nag Hammadi. Québec
BKV	Bibliothek der Kirchenväter. München
CCL	Corpus christianorum, series Latina
CH	Church History. Chicago
CSCO	Corpus scriptorum christianorum orientalium
CSEL	Corpus scriptorum ecclesiasticorum latinorum
D	Denzinger-Schönmetzer, Enchiridion symbolorum definitionum et declarationum de rebus fidei et morum
DHGE	Dictionnaire d'histoire et de géographie ecclésiastiques. Paris
DS	Dictionnaire de spiritualité. Paris
FC	Fathers of the Church
GCS	Die griechischen christlichen Schriftsteller der ersten Jahrhunderte
HE	Eusebius, Historia ecclesiastica
HTR	Harvard Theological Review. Cambridge (Mass.)
In Jo.	Origen, Commentary on John
In Matth.	Origen, Commentary on Matthew
JEH	Journal of Ecclesiastical History. London
JR	The Journal of Religion. Chicago
JTS	Journal of Theological Studies. Oxford
MTZ	Münchener theologische Zeitschrift. München

NHS	Nag Hammadi Studies. Leiden
NT	Novum Testamentum. Leiden
Pan.	Epiphanius, Panarion (see chapter III, note 8)
PG	Patrologia graeca
PL	Patrologia latina
PO	Patrologia orientalis
RAC	Reallexikon für Antike und Christentum. Stuttgart
Ref.	Hippolytus, Refutatio omnium haeresium (or Elenchos) (see chapter II, notes 1 and 2)
RHE	Revue d'histoire ecclésiastique. Louvain
RHPR	Revue d'histoire et de philosophie religieuses. Paris
RHR	Revue de l'histoire des religions. Paris
RSPT	Revue des sciences philosophiques et théologiques. Paris
RechSR	Recherches de science religieuse. Paris
RevSR	Revue des sciences religieuses. Strasbourg
RTAM	Revue de théologie ancienne et mediévale. Louvain
RThPh	Revue de théologie et de philosophie. Lausanne
SC	Sources chrétiennes
Str.	Clement of Alexandria, Stromateis
StTh	Studia theologica. Oslo
TLZ	Theologische Literaturzeitung. Berlin
TR	Theologische Revue. Münster
TrTZ	Trierer theologische Zeitschrift. Trier
TU	Texte und Untersuchungen zur Geschichte der altchristlichen Literatur
TZ	Theologische Zeitschrift. Basel
VC	Vigiliae christianae. Amsterdam
ZKG	Zeitschrift für Kirchengeschichte. Stuttgart

ZNW   Zeitschrift für die neutestamentliche Wissenschaft. Berlin

ZTK   Zeitschrift für Theologie und Kirche. Tübingen

INTRODUCTION: HERESIOLOGY AND NORMATIVE CHRISTIANITY

The study presented here is devoted to three early Christian heresiologists and their works: Irenaeus of Lyons, who wrote his Adversus haereses around 180; Hippolytus of Rome, who is generally held to be the author of the Elenchos Against All Heresies, written after 222; and Epiphanius of Salamis, whose Panarion against eighty heresies was written between 374 and 377. Before posing the question that will be at the center of our investigation, it may be in order to offer a few preliminary remarks about the study of heresiology in general and of these three heresiological works in particular.

1. Why study heresiology? What truth can we hope to wring from the most intransigent authors of the Christian tradition, those most inclined to 'satanize' their adversaries? Do we not now possess far more reliable knowledge of ancient heresies from the Nag Hammadi finds and the ensuing revival of gnostic studies? Can we not now dispense with the 'biased' witness of the Church Fathers?

This is a reasonable question, but any satisfactory answer is bound to be complex. Although the Nag Hammadi discoveries--and the resulting scholarship--are important for our knowledge of the religious history of the patristic period, the heresiologists have by no means been supplanted. On the contrary, they represent a largely independent source of data to guide the historian's inquiry. The heresiologists drew on sources other than, though sometimes similar to, the Nag Hammadi texts. And if the patristic evidence must be complemented and corrected by the direct evidence of heterodox writings, these writings offer too scattered and fragmentary a fund of information to permit, by themselves, a satisfactory reconstruction of the heterodoxy they represent. (Of

course, the patristic evidence itself ought to be
complemented by the new sources, thereby ridding it of some
of its one-sidedness; but we do not have to belabor this
view since it is most vigorously expressed today.) It is
important to recall that the context provided by the
heresiologists is broader than that of the Nag Hammadi
texts; that the heresiologists, for all their one-
sidedness, offer us valuable attempts to conceptualize
gnosis; and that, for these reasons, the heresiological
writings remain indispensable for the interpretation of
these new sources.[1]

   In fact, Nag Hammadi studies frequently refer to the
evidence of the Church Fathers in the attempt to assess the
meaning of the newly discovered texts. Scholars regularly
look for parallel information, especially in Irenaeus,
Hippolytus, and Epiphanius, demonstrating that the new
sources have not superseded the heresiologists.

   In any effort to gain a better knowledge of ancient
heresy from the heresiologists, however, a preliminary
condition has to be borne in mind. Information on heresies
found in heresiological works, particularly on the gnostic
heresies which interest us here, is embedded in an anti-
heretical argument. This mode of argument always reflects
the particular concerns of each heresiologist. If we want
to assess properly the value of the information thus
provided, especially when the author is not explicitly
quoting a source, it is necessary to be as clear as
possible about the concerns of the heresiologists and about
the nature of the arguments they wish to oppose to the
heretics.

   Although a better knowledge of heresiology undoubtedly
improves the quality of our knowledge of ancient heresies,

---

[1]The same point is forcefully emphasized by H.-M.
Schenke, 'Die Relevanz der Kirchenväter für die
Erschliessung der Nag-Hammadi Texte', Das Korpus der
griechischen christlichen Schriftsteller. Historie,
Gegenwart, Zukunft, eds. J. Irmscher and K. Treu, TU 120,
Berlin 1977, pp. 209-218.

the study of heresiology as a literary genre is,
surprisingly enough, a rather neglected field. P. Nautin
has already remarked: 'S'il existe de bonnes études sur
les procédés ordinaires de l'hagiographie et les risques
qu'elle comporte pour l'histoire exacte, nous n'avons
malheureusement rien de tel pour l'hérésiologie'.[2] The
present study does not pretend to answer the implied
invitation to pay close attention to the methods of
heresiology; rather, it echoes in its own way the same
invitation.

The question of 'heretics' has an ominous relevance to
our day.[3] 'Heresy' is no longer used in an exclusively
religious sense, but the analogy between ancient heretics
and contemporary minorities struggling for survival is too
striking to be overlooked or dismissed. The struggle over
meaning in our world and the hardly less bitter battles
between the orthodox and the heretics in Christian
antiquity are reciprocally illuminating. If ideological
conflict today is a life-and-death issue, so was the issue
of religious truth for early Christianity.

We also wish to emphasize the relevance of heresiology
to the question of what people thought Christianity stood
for[4]. We must not expect to find in heresiological

---

[2]P. Nautin, 'Histoire des dogmes et des sacrements
chrétiens', Problèmes et méthodes d'histoire des religions
(École pratique des Hautes Études, Section Sciences
religieuses), Paris 1968, pp. 177-191, here p. 183.   In
Mélanges d'histoire des religions offerts à H.-C. Puech,
Paris 1974, pp. 393-403 ('Les fragments de Basilide sur la
souffrance'), Nautin remarks again that our better
knowledge of Gnosticism depends not only on the
availability of gnostic texts, but also on a better
analysis of the method of heresiologists (see p. 393).

[3]See G. Hasenhüttl and J. Nolte, Formen kirchlicher
Ketzerbewältigung, Düsseldorf 1976, p. 11.

[4]Origen, Contra Celsum 3, 13 (H. Chadwick, ed.,
Cambridge 1953, p. 136) said something similar about the
heresies themselves when he saw in the necessary
development of sects a fortunate expression of the richness
of Christianity and of its essential features: 'I would

writings 'the truth about the Gnostics'; too often in these
writings the information is tainted by passion or woven
within an alien argument that obscures it. Nor can we
expect to draw from such writings a ready-made account of
'history as it actually happened'; for here, more than
ever, the data are decisively placed within an
interpretative scheme that colours them. But we can hope
to find in those writings what certain influential authors
in the emergence of catholic Christianity considered to be
the pivotal point on which Christianity would stand or
fall, and how they acted to secure that point. Each
heresiologist, to be sure, had his own view of 'the essence
of Christianity'. It may have reflected social, cultural,
and political preferences and idiosyncracies.
Collectively, in any case, these views had a momentous
impact on the shaping of tradition. In this context it is
worth our while to ask what the diverse views of
heresiologists were and whether there was any continuity
between them.

Let these reflections suffice as a justification for
the study of the heresiologists in general. A further
question arises: out of the large number of heresiologists
who wrote during the first centuries, why concentrate on
the Adversus haereses of Irenaeus, the Elenchos of
Hippolytus, and the Panarion of Epiphanius? The answer, in
a nutshell, is that these works are available; they are
typical; and they each took on 'all the heresies' of their
own day.

They are available – that is, they survived. Justin
wrote a Syntagma dealing also with all heresies and so did
Hippolytus. Unfortunately, both are lost, and efforts to
reconstruct them have obviously not succeeded in giving
them back to us in their entirety. At best we might

---

say that a man who looks carefully into the sects of
Judaism and Christianity becomes a very wise Christian'
(σοφώτατον).

identify generically the heresies they refuted and infer
something of the influence of these now lost works on the
history of heresiology. It is not possible, however, to
gain a clear idea of the arguments they used to counter
their opponents. For that reason these works fall beyond
the scope of our interests in the present study.

Second, the Adversus haereses, the Elenchos, and the
Panarion are typical representatives of the literary genre
called 'heresiology'. These works offer us excellent
illustrations of what heresiology was in three successive
centuries, and they allow us to follow the development of
heresiology in that period. Moreover, they had a decisive
and lasting influence on the fixing of the style of
Christian polemics. Their respective sources or their
interdependence are not of primary concern here, although
at times it will be useful to indicate the probable source
of their ideas; but our main interest is in the authors
themselves. Each is seen as representing one major moment
in the heresiological tradition.

Third, all three did battle with all heresies they
knew, not only with particular heresies. This
distinguishes them from heresiologists like Tertullian,
Theophilus of Antioch, or Origen who took aim at one or
another chosen target (Marcion or the Valentinians).

After Epiphanius heresiology betrays a depletion of
energies. Pseudo-Tertullian, Filastrius of Brescia,
Theodoret of Cyrus, also writing against all heresies, rely
primarily for their information on Hippolytus's Syntagma.
Filastrius and Theodoret do not directly depend on
Epiphanius; they rather parallel him, and do not expand our
knowledge of early heresies. The same may be said of
Augustine; he knew the 'Anakephalaioseis' of the Panarion
and it is on them that he based his information in his De
haeresibus. After Epiphanius no fresh knowledge of ancient
heresies can be expected.[5] New methods of dealing with

---

[5]I venture the following chart, based on Lipsius,
Hilgenfeld and others, showing the 'genealogy' of

heretics will indeed be developed. But a study of these
methods would include medieval heresiology up to the
Reformation, which is beyond the scope of the present
study. We are interested here in understanding the methods
of dealing with ancient heresies.

2. The scope of our study has now emerged. We do not
intend, in such a limited space, to present a comprehensive
study of these three authors, nor a detailed analysis of
some specific passages of their works; nor to bring into
our study all the rich new information on the Gnostics
produced in the wake of Nag Hammadi, although we do think
that our discussion has some relevance to Nag Hammadi
studies. We intend to address a precise question to the
three heresiological works considered in themselves.

---

heresiologists and the central position of the three
authors we study here.
'Q' would be a reworking of Justin's Syntagma (according to
Lipsius);
⟶ indicates that the contact is well attested;
- - - - - - - - indicates that the contact is probable.
Further explanations will be provided by the following
chapters.

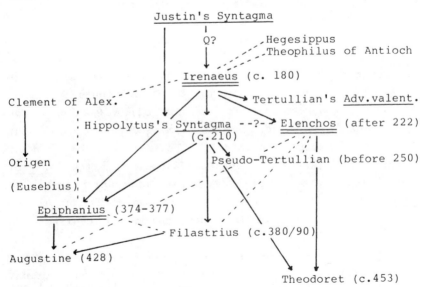

Beyond all literary devices, rhetorical or other, encountered in these writings, we wish to determine the substance of the arguments forged by each heresiologist to counter the Gnostics. We are not primarily interested in reaching a clear picture of the opponents each heresiologist is attacking; like the actual descriptions of sects, the kind of arguments marshalled against them sometimes indeed betrays who the heresiologist thought his opponents were. Nevertheless we want to probe elsewhere in an effort to uncover the central argument that each writer has devised in order to overthrow heresy. Thereby we assume that the many arguments encountered in each work are informed by a prevailing argument; it is our objective to isolate such an argument. In order to find an answer to our question, it is also implied that we have to answer the essentially connected question: what did each heresiologist find most offensive in the heretical positions?

If we can come close to answering such questions, we will have gained a deeper knowledge of the development of the style of Christian polemics in the first centuries. Also the essential content and motive of such polemics might emerge in a fuller light; for what each heresiologist sadly misses in the combatted doctrines is very likely to stand close to what he holds to be the backbone of Christianity.

The present study was undertaken in the context of a research project on Normative Self-Definition in Judaism and Christianity. The project was funded by the Social Sciences and Humanities Research Council of Canada and was based in the Department of Religious Studies at McMaster University. The reader is therefore invited to keep in mind that the heuristic and controlling framework of this study has been one determined by the question of the emergence of orthodox Christianity. I have intended in it to do my part in a corporate attempt to understand and explain how and why normative Christianity developed in precisely the way in which it did. The Conclusion will

reconsider this broader question in the light of the
results of the preceding chapters.

I. IRENAEUS'S REFUTATION OF THE GNOSTICS

Irenaeus of Lyons (c.130-202) wrote his refutation of heresies,[1] principally gnostic heresies, at a time (beginning c. 180) when gnostic groups were still perceived as a dangerous presence, if not as a threat to the very existence of the Church. The Rhone valley had been, and still was, the place where gnostic activists, above all Marcosian Gnostics, had made headway and won many converts from the Church. Irenaeus knew them personally; he supposedly had 'conversations' with them, and had read some of their writings. On the other hand, Irenaeus had predecessors in the task of overthrowing heretics and it is generally assumed that he knew the lost Syntagma of Justin, among other heresiological sources. Thus, on account of his knowledge of both heresy and heresiology, he seemed to have been well equipped to speak out against the 'Gnosis falsely so-called', the more so if one considers that his function as a bishop gave him the responsibility of speaking a word of warning and speaking it with authority.

---

[1] Ἐλέγχου καὶ ἀνατροπῆς τῆς ψευδωνύμου γνώσεως βιβλία πέντε (according to Eusebius, HE V, 7) — Detectionis et eversionis falso cognominatae agnitionis seu contra omnes haereses libri quinque (= Adv. haer.). We quote the work in the following way: for the text we follow W.W. Harvey's edition (Cambridge 1857) and SC 263-264, 210-211, 100 (2 vols.), 152-153 (eds. A. Rousseau, J. Doutreleau, C. Mercier, B. Hemmerdinger, Paris 1979, 1974, 1965, 1969) for Books I, III, IV and V. (Book II is forthcoming in SC series.) — For the divisions of the text we follow P. Massuet (PG 7), whose divisions are reproduced by A. Stieren (Leipzig 1853) and SC, while they can be found in the margins of Harvey's edition. Our translation takes account of those found in ANF I (Edinburgh 1867) and SC. A new English translation is expected to appear in "Fathers of the Church" (Washington) by A.C. Way and in "Ancient Christian Writers" (Washington) by D. Unger.

Throughout the five Books of Adversus haereses (Adv.haer.) and especially in the Prefaces to each Book, Irenaeus refers to a 'friend' who expressed the wish to know more about the heretics[2] of the time (i.e. first of all the Valentinians), and to hear how to oppose them successfully. Attempts at identifying that 'friend' are doomed to failure. For nothing indicates that he was another bishop. He might even not have been the 'lettre influent' Doutreleau thinks he was,[3] for if that were the case, Irenaeus might have given more weight than he did to philosophical considerations. The 'friend' might be fictitious, or stand for a segment of Irenaeus's community which was disturbed by gnostic agitations and wished to be in a better position to discern among those teachings and defend itself. But even granted that the 'friend' was a real addressee and an influential person, he does not appear to have had any official status in the Church.

Thus Adv.haer. does not present itself as an officially commissioned work. Rather Irenaeus saw the danger represented by the activity of gnostic teachers in his entourage and stood up as a pastor concerned with true teaching.[4] Without being asked by his peers to write a tractate against the 'Gnosis falsely so-called', he took it

---

[2]On the use of the term 'Gnostics' by early heresiologists, see N. Brox,' Γνωστικοί als häresiologischer Terminus', ZNW 57, 1966, pp. 105-114. On self-designations of the Gnostics, see K. Rudolph, Die Gnosis. Wesen und Geschichte einer spätantiken Religion, Göttingen 1977, pp. 220-221. On the use of the term in Adv. haer. I, see A. Rousseau, Irénée de Lyon. Contre les hérésies, Livre I (SC 263), Paris 1979, pp. 299-300.

[3]L. Doutreleau, 'Irénée de Lyon', DS VII, Paris 1971, 1933. A. Rousseau (SC 263, p. 115 n. 1) suggests, on the basis of Adv. haer. I. praef. 2 and I.31.4 ('omnibus his qui sunt tecum'): 'Peut-être s'agit-il du chef d'une communauté chrétienne...'.

[4]Irenaeus would be among the first writers in the West who tried to unite the authority of a bishop with that of a teacher. See W. Bousset, Jüdisch-christlicher Schulbetrieb in Alexandria und Rom, Göttingen 1915, p. 317. Looking

upon himself to show to his people (naturally with an eye
to an eventual wider audience) what is right and true.
'The true gnosis is the doctrine of the apostles'
(IV.33.8).   Irenaeus, viewing himself in line with the
apostles and the primitive Church, writes to establish this
fact and, at the same time, to vindicate his own
authority.

But there was something more constructive and creative
in Irenaeus's speaking out.   He wrote at a time when the
heretic/orthodox polarization does not seem to have been
clear.[5]   The tractates written by Theophilus of Antioch and
Justin against divergent teachings would not have effected
a clear line of demarcation between contending parties;
gnostic teachers could still move freely among Christians
many years after these tractates were written, even in
Rome.   What Irenaeus achieved, at least in the West, was
not only the intended refutation, but the lasting
polarization of Christian fronts.

How did Irenaeus achieve this?   Why did he feel he had
to speak out?   What gave him the assurance that he was
right?   Why did he attack the Gnostics in the way he did?
What was the character of the arguments he used in order to
'compel the animal to break cover,...not only expose the
wild beast to view, but inflict wounds upon it from every
side', and 'finally slay that destructive brute' (I.31.4)?

---

back at the second century, Danielou, Origène (Paris 1948,
p. 37), says concerning Origen's difficulties with the
bishop Demetrius: 'Nous retrouvons là cette distinction du
courant hiérarchique et du courant des didascales qui
s'était rencontrée au IIe siècle.   Les rapports entre les
deux n'étaient pas encore bien définis dans l'Église'.   The
emerging of orthodoxy will be the triumph of the bishops
and, with them, assuredly of the 'majority'.

[5]This can be said without contradicting, among others,
H. J. Carpenter ('Popular Christianity and the Theologians
in the Early Centuries', JTS 14, 1963, pp. 294-310), who
holds that '...Irenaeus and Tertullian and Hippolytus dealt
with Marcion and the Gnostics when the great church had
demonstrably survived the impact of these movements for
half a century or more' (p. 297).

Such questions will guide our inquiry into Irenaeus's
motives for writing his refutation.

An analysis of Irenaeus's work clearly shows two
groups of arguments which he himself characterizes as
philosophical and scriptural/theological. But a third
group, which we shall call socio-political, although less
explicitly put forward, is nevertheless operative and might
have given the initial stimulus to Irenaeus's enterprise.
The first two groups of arguments have already been studied
by many authors; my intention in presenting them here is to
offer as comprehensive a view of Irenaeus's refutation as
possible, and to provide necessary background for the third
group.

1. Philosophical Arguments

The refutation proper of the gnostic system (of their
regula: II.praef. 2) begins with Book II where most of
Irenaeus's philosophical arguments are found. Here the
order of the 'headings' corresponds to the order of the
presentation of the gnostic tenets in Book I. But it
should be noted that the 'exposition' of the gnostic
'hypothesis' in Book I was itself intended to show its lack
of internal cohesion. This constituted the first stage of
Irenaeus's refutation (I.31.3: 'Simply to exhibit their
sentiments, is to obtain a victory over them.').

We shall not follow step by step the argumentation
which aims at showing that the gnostic system does not
harmonize 'with what actually exists or with right reason'
(II.25.1), nor with human experience (II.27,1), nor with
common sense (II.26.3; see I.16.3). We shall, however,
make some general observations on the character of the
philosophical arguments found here and in other parts of
Adv.haer.

Throughout his refutation, Irenaeus shows acquaintance
with secular learning and especially with the rhetorical
arguments and techniques of the Hellenistic schools of the

second century.[6] The very order of the arguments in Books
II to V betrays such an acquaintance, for it was a common
rhetorical technique to hold back the decisive arguments
for the later parts of the development and to present the
weaker ones first. Irenaeus follows this pattern by
presenting first his philosophical arguments against the
Gnostics and then by offering the more decisive scriptural
arguments.

More precisely, Irenaeus's rhetorical training (which
he might have received in Rome) is seen in the fact that he
uses almost all methods of argumentation (except the
syllogism, as Reynders noted),[7] with a predilection for the
dilemma and the question. The principles he uses are
simple, almost commonplaces. For example: 'The one who
conceives is also the one who makes'; 'cause contains
effect'; 'what is prior contains what is posterior'; etc.[8]
He excels in the use of irony and the ad hominem retort,
thus showing a certain talent and training.[9]

Irenaeus's acquaintance with philosophy itself 'is
somewhat superficial'.[10] He surely can formulate an
argument; but what is properly philosophical in his work
seems to be for the most part drawn from doxographical

---

[6]See W. R. Schoedel, 'Philosophy and Rhetoric in the
Adversus Haereses of Irenaeus', VC 13, 1959, pp. 22-32,
esp. 27-32. R. M. Grant, 'Irenaeus and Hellenistic
Culture', HTR 42, 1949, pp. 41-51, esp. 47-51. P. Perkins,
'Irenaeus and the Gnostics. Rhetoric and Composition in
Adversus Haereses Book One', VC 30, 1976, pp. 193-200.

[7]D. B. Reynders, 'La polémique de saint Irénée.
Méthode et principes', RTAM 7, 1935, pp. 5-27, here p. 8.

[8]See Reynders, 'Polémique'.

[9]See R. M. Grant, 'Irenaeus', p. 51: 'Too often we
are content with a picture of Irenaeus as orthodox but
rather stupid. The camera needs to be refocussed...He
represents the confluence of Hellenism and Christianity no
less distinctly than the apologists do...He should not be
neglected simply because his results survived'.

[10]Schoedel, 'Philosophy and Rhetoric', p. 22; see p.
31.

materials, i.e. from essentially eclectic sources.[11]   The
rest of his thought could be characterized as popular
philosophy.[12]   This is precisely the area where Irenaeus
seems to be most at ease.   At least that type of wisdom
harmonizes well with the praise of simple faith that is
found throughout Adv.haer.   The most typical and frequent
arguments of Irenaeus belong to this category of popular
philosophy. Some examples might suffice to illustrate this
point.

Irenaeus's favourite refrain is: the Gnostics are
talking nonsense, folly; their discourse departs from good
sense; they 'fall into a fit of frenzy', they propound
'fictitious doctrines'; they are seriously sick and foolish
(see I.16.3). Their teaching is absurd and their exegesis,
arbitrary (II.24.1-6).

The accusation that gnostic teachings are borrowed
from philosophy (II.14.2-7; see IV.33.3) is itself meant to
disqualify them. Plagiarizing the philosophers is not a
good recommendation in Christian matters, since, for
Irenaeus, philosophy is at the source of wrong doctrines.
There is only one passage in which Irenaeus commends a
philosopher--Plato--but it is only to say that Plato is
more religious than Marcion (III.25.5).   This surely does
not amount in Irenaeus's eyes to a praise of philosophy.
But Valentinian speculation is not only taken from the
philosophers: it is philosophy.   Gnosis describes
philosophical or psychological processes which it takes for
real entities (II.14.6 and 8; II.13.10; II.28.6);[13] making

---

[11]One source is probably the Pseudo-Plutarch.   See
Schoedel, 'Philosophy and Rhetoric', pp. 23-4; Grant,
'Irenaeus', pp. 43-7: 'Irenaeus cannot be classified among
philosophical schools.   His interest...is more rhetorical
than philosophical' (p. 47).

[12]See, for instance, his use of proverbs (II.19.8);
his appeal to the authority of the past, e.g. Plato; his
appeal to universal opinion; the sceptical use he makes of
the doxographical material.

[13]See F.-M.-M. Sagnard, La gnose valentinienne et le

dangerous and excessive use of human analogies, it hypostasizes mental processes. In addition to these accusations a series of denunciations of the 'gnosis falsely so-called' is found. Gnostics contradict the facts or right reason; their teachings are recent, originating from Simon who is not only despicable, but also a novator (II.28.8 'recens'); they are therefore less respectable than ancient teachings; they are subtle, without simplicity;[14] Gnostics disagree between themselves and, lacking practical knowledge and virtue, they display only cowardice.[15]

---

témoignage de saint Irénée, Paris 1947, pp. 281ff., 321 n. 1, 410.

[14]See M. Widmann, 'Irenäus und seine theologischen Väter', ZTK 54, 1957, pp. 156-73, esp. 172f. On the features of Irenaeus's polemic see N. Brox, 'Antignostische Polemik bei Christen und Heiden', MTZ 18, 1967, pp. 265-91.

[15]W. H. C. Frend states that the Gnostics 'faded out at the time of the Great Persecution, and their place is immediately taken by the Manichees', in Africa at least: Frend, 'The Gnostic-Manichaean Tradition in Roman North Africa', JEH 4, 1953, pp. 13-26, here p. 15. In another article, Frend writes that Gnostics, because of their readiness to syncretism and to compromise with the Greco-Roman civilization, 'were not generally molested'. ('The Gnostic Sects and the Roman Empire', JEH 5, 1954, pp. 25-37, here p. 28.) The fact that Gnostics least resembled the synagogue both in its ethic and in its outlook towards the Gentiles (p. 26) and did not show the form of religious exclusiveness characteristic of the synagogue and the church accounts for the relative peace Gnostics enjoyed. Frend is led to the conclusion that 'in the first two centuries the persecutions were confined to one type of Christian who might reasonably be called "the new Israel"' (p. 35): those men and women had been schooled to regard persecution as their lot. It is to this view that W. Ullmann ('Gnostische und politische Häresie bei Celsus', Theologische Versuche II [eds. J. Rogge und G. Schille], Berlin 1970, pp. 153-58) seems to take exception when he suggests that we should investigate more carefully '[nach] möglichen Zusammenhängen zwischen gnostischer Lehre und einem Bild des Christentums bei seinen Gegnern..., das Verfolgung provozieren musste'. We shall return to this point below.

Only a few of these assertions have real philosophical significance. We find many agreements between Irenaeus and Plotinus in the critique of the Gnostics; but nothing is found in Irenaeus that has the philosophical character of the argumentation put forward by Plotinus in _Enn_. II.9 (see Porphyry, _Vita Plotini_ 16). If one persists in calling Irenaeus's arguments at this point philosophical, they should be qualified as popular philosophy or popular wisdom.[16]   They do not, in themselves, constitute the overthrow of Gnosis that has been promised. Irenaeus seems to agree that his philosophical arguments are not that decisive; otherwise Irenaeus the rhetorician would not have presented them at the outset, thus conceding their relative weakness.

2.   Theological Arguments

The decisive arguments must be theological or scriptural. Here Irenaeus uses all the resources available to him from his predecessors and adds an original contribution.

Among the many theological arguments that Irenaeus mounts against the Gnostics there are a few that are constantly repeated. These can obviously lead us to what Irenaeus thought was at stake in the debate.

Turning against the Gnostics the accusation of ignorance they address to ordinary Christians, Irenaeus accuses them of ignoring God's dispensation, the rule of faith, scripture and tradition. In a word, they ignore the 'hypothesis' of truth, substance of the Christian faith. P. Hefner has pointed out how crucial this concept of 'hypothesis' is to Irenaeus's refutation.[17] It designates

---

[16]See P. Perkins, 'Irenaeus and the Gnostics'.

[17]P. Hefner, 'Theological Methodology and St. Irenaeus', JR 44, 1964, pp. 294-309. According to Hefner (p. 295) 'the one highest authority' that stands out in Irenaeus's work 'is the system, framework, or "hypothesis"

the 'organic system or framework which constitutes the
shape and meaning of God's revelation'. In a formal sense,
it functions as the ultimate norm of truth and encompasses
all other norms: it includes God's economy of redemption,
is rooted in God, announced by the prophets, taught by the
Lord, delivered by the apostles;   it is derived from
scripture and also serves to expound scripture; it resides
in the community of the Church and reaches the community
through tradition; it is summarized in creedlike statements
and can be expounded by reason. The hypothesis of truth is
the ultimate authority which guides Irenaeus's criticism
and to which all other authorities are subordinated.[18]
Concretely applied by Irenaeus to meet the gnostic
assertions, it is in practice equivalent to the 'rule' that
there is one God, creator of the world, Father of our Lord
Jesus Christ, and author of the economy (I.10.1).[19]

---

of the Faith whose substance is comprised in God's
redemptive dispensation on man's behalf'. This is the
authority which holds together all others and to which all
others are subordinated: scripture, tradition, church,
bishop, creed and revelation. Hefner's study of the notion
of 'hypothesis' of truth as essential for the enucleation
of Irenaeus's theological methodology ends with the
suggestion that 'closer attention be paid to the concept of
regula fidei' (p. 302). Reynders ('Polémique', pp. 16-7)
had already seen the ultimate norm of authority for
Irenaeus as being that 'synthèse doctrinale' which is 'le
corps de vérité'.   On the meaning of 'hypothesis' see
recently W. C. van Unnik, 'An Interesting Document of the
Second Century Theological Discussion', VC 31, 1977, pp.
196-228, esp. 206-208.

[18]The question of legitimate authority is crucial to
Irenaeus's refutation; the emphasis he puts on authority
gives his theology its specific character. However, after
Hefner's contribution it should have become impossible to
pit the authorities whom Irenaeus considers normative
against each other.

[19]The proximity of the notion of 'hypothesis' to that
of the 'rule of faith' appears in N. Brox's description of
the rule as 'Inbegriff dessen, was er [Irenäus] für
heilsnotwendig, für tatsächlich geschehen, von Gott
geoffenbart und darum für unüberbietbar hält'.
Offenbarung, Gnosis und Gnostischer Mythos bei Irenäus von
Lyon, Salzburg/München 1966, p. 113.   See also B. Hägglund,

For this hypothesis of faith, the Gnostics substitute their own hypothesis which they 'dreamt into existence' (I.9.3). Obviously the hypothesis of faith is radically subverted if another God is conceived beyond the Creator. Thus Gnostics distort God's revelation and destroy the faith of the pious. Thereby they replace real salvific acts by their own inventions, fictions, and jugglings (I.15.5), practicing a sort of theology-fiction, projecting mental processes into an atemporal framework[20] which develops into an arbitrary speculation about the Pleroma and its aeons and amounts to an utterly indiscrete theologia gloriae. In so doing, they not only deceive the simple believers, but also show that they do not care about the apostolic tradition which they do not possess. This leads men to despair about their salvation (IV.praef.4)[21] and ultimately to deny salvation. For the gnostic view of salvation does not include the flesh; but if the flesh is not saved, nothing of man is saved (II.29.3; V.6-7; V.20.1).

Thus Gnostics freely subtract from and add to the hypothesis of truth.[22] This arbitrariness is not only opposed to Irenaeus's temperament and his positivist

---

'Die Bedeutung der "regula fidei" als Grundlage theologischer Aussagen', StTh 12, 1958, pp. 1-44; A. Rousseau and J. Doutreleau, eds., Irénée de Lyon. Contre les hérésies, Livre III (SC 210), Paris 1974, pp. 220-21.

[20]See Sagnard, Gnose valentinienne, pp. 259, 571.

[21]See Reynders, 'Optimisme et théocentrisme chez saint Irénée', RTAM 8, 1936, pp. 225-52, esp. 252.

[22]Reynders ('Optimisme', pp. 229-30) has collected the expressions used by Irenaeus to describe how casually the Gnostics deal with truth: adaptare, assimilare, adulterare, calumniantes, transvertentes, abutentes, transferunt, auferentes, transfingunt, transfigurant, transformantes, solvens, compingentes, confingentes, figmentum, transfictio, fictio, in captivitatem ducunt a veritate, falsi testes, frustrantur speciem evangelii, circumcidentes evangelium, eligentes, decurtantes, intercidentes deminoraverunt. See N. Brox, Offenbarung, p. 197, on this 'heillose Automonie' of the Gnostics.

emphasis on the clear and real facts of the economy,[23] it
is also blasphemous.[24]

With the accusation of 'blasphemy'[25] cast at the
Gnostics by Irenaeus we come to the core of his theological
objections, for this accusation, in its context, sums up
what he thinks about the Valentinians: they render men
'disbelievers in their own salvation, and blasphemous
against God who shaped them' (IV.praef.4). They are guilty
of blasphemy because they destroy the substance of the
faith; their very thinking about God is blasphemous
(IV.praef.3) because it introduces divisions into God; it
splits the divine and breaks its unity (II.28.2 and 8).
Moreover Gnostics introduce such divisions throughout the
real.   They distinguish between God and the Creator,
between Christ and Christ, between different 'economies',
etc. The division of the divine is the point which upsets
Irenaeus most;[26] it is above all expressed in the

---

[23]On the positivist character of the 'true gnosis'
(and also of the rule of faith), see N. Brox, Offenbarung,
pp. 179-89, 196-99; Hägglund, 'Bedeutung'.

[24]This view is widespread in antiquity: adding to or
subtracting from a received tradition is considered to be
blasphemous.   See W. C. van Unnik, 'De la règle
Μήτε προσθεῖναι μήτε ἀφελεῖν dans l'histoire du canon',
VC 3, 1949, pp. 1-36, esp. pp. 32-5. This 'rule' is found
above all in texts coming from Asia Minor, Irenaeus's place
of origin: see ibid., pp. 9, 36. Irenaeus (I.10.2-3)
strongly emphasizes that faith is one and the same; it
cannot be augmented by those who have a greater degree of
intelligence, nor diminished by those who are less gifted.

[25]A similar accusation is also found in Plotinus, Enn.
II.9.16.

[26]See R. A. Markus, 'Pleroma and Fulfilment. The
Significance of History in St. Irenaeus' Opposition to
Gnosticism', VC 8, 1954, pp. 193-224, esp. p. 212. Against
the breaking up of the divine Irenaeus makes the case of
unity, which is the main theme of Adv. haer.   See A.
Benoit, Saint Irénée.   Introduction à l'étude de sa
théologie, Paris 1960, pp. 203-205:   'Le thème que la
lecture de l'ouvrage Contre les hérésies accentue avec le
plus de force est celui de l'unité...Par cette affirmation
de l'unité, Irénée relève le défi que lui lance la gnose.
Car l'essence de cette dernière, c'est le morcellement, la

denigrating of the God of the Old Testament. Irenaeus
repeatedly counters the gnostic devaluation of the Old
Testament God by insisting on the unity of God and the
Creator and by affirming the truth and reality of the Old
Testament God. This 'Ringen um den Status des AT Gottes'[27]
is to Irenaeus of utmost importance.

The blasphemous split of the divine introduced by the
Gnostics is the starting point for Irenaeus's attack
against their dualistic teaching. From that point Irenaeus
will investigate the many facets and expressions of gnostic
dualism. Dualism will thus become the target of his
attack.

Irenaeus, making a case for the unity which is truth
and which lies in the Church goes through all the forms of
dualism, rejecting each one. First of all, he attacks the
'morcellement du divin' which we may call theological
dualism: i.e., the split between God and the demiurge,
which is the central point of his attack. He also attacks
the division between the good God and the just God and the
division of the divine in the Pleroma expressed by the
doctrine of Aeons. 'Such divisions cannot be ascribed to
God' (II.28.4); they suppress the deity (III.25.3). God is
one: the identity of God the Creator and God the Father is
the central article of Irenaeus's creed and the sum of his
argument (see II.31.1, where he summarizes his
argument).[28]

---

division, le dualisme...Il y a vu lui-même la réponse à
l'hérésie'.

[27]N. Brox, Offenbarung, pp. 48-9. See W. Ullmann
('Gnostische und politische Häresie', p. 155), for whom the
central difference between the Great Church and Gnosis
resides in their 'gegensätzliche Stellung zu dem Gott der
Juden'.

[28]Irenaeus is among those who cannot tolerate the idea
that creation and universe could be the work of an ignorant
or imperfect demiurge (improvident, negligent, incapable,
indifferent, powerless, capricious or jealous), or the
result of a downfall or of a deficiency; he cannot bear the
idea that human life could be a prey to a 'mauvais génie'.

From this central article of his creed two further articles are derived: one Christ, one economy. Irenaeus sees the Christological dualism, separating Christ from Jesus (IV.praef.3; IV.2.4; III.16.2; III.17.4; etc.), the Logos from the Saviour (III.9.3; III.16.8; IV.praef.3; etc.), the Christ above from the Christ below (III.11.1; III.17.4; etc.), as a typical gnostic affirmation and as a blasphemy as well (IV.praef.3). This he attacks, as well as the soteriological dualism, whereby the universality of God's economy and will for salvation is denied.[29] There is only one economy, which is universal, and on the basis of which Christ will recapitulate all things.[30]

We may enumerate other forms of dualism to which Irenaeus objects: Scriptural dualism, which separates the NT from the OT and ultimately the God of the OT from the God announced by the Savior, against which Irenaeus affirms the unity and 'harmony' of the two convenants. Ecclesiastical dualism, according to which a distinction is made between simple believers and pneumatics, thus breaking the unity of the Church.

> [The spiritual disciple] shall also judge
> those who give rise to schisms...and who for

This would ruin the idea of providence and that of human freedom, ideas central to religious thought in the 2nd and 3rd century. Gnostic dualism introduces into these ideas an element which creates anxiety since it implies that 'Gott als König herrscht, aber nicht regiert', and that therefore 'die Herrschaft Gottes zwar gut, aber die Regierung des Demiurgen...schlecht ist' (E. Peterson, Der Monotheismus als politisches Problem, Leipzig 1935, pp. 20-1). Irenaeus's parti-pris for optimism, which is not based on philosophy and which represents a form of instinctive humanism, leads him to counter all that threatens order in universe and life. See Reynders, 'Optimisme'. It should be noted here that, while Irenaeus finds comfort in the idea that the Creator is close to the world, Gnostics despise the Creator precisely because of his proximity to the world.

[29]See Brox, Offenbarung, p. 178.

[30]See Benoit, Saint Irénée, pp. 219-27.

> trifling reasons, or any kind of reason
> which occurs to them, cut in pieces and
> divide the great and glorious body of
> Christ, and so far as in them lies, destroy
> it...For no reformation of so great
> importance can be effected by them, as will
> compensate for the mischief arising from
> their schism (IV.33.7; see IV.26.2).[31]

Social dualism, whereby some are said to be good, others
evil, by nature (IV.37.2), which Irenaeus sees as
contradicting the equality of all men before God's offer[32]
and as threatening the unity of the church and its peace.
Practical dualism, according to which some recommend, over
against the common discipline, either the rigorism
attainable only by a few or the libertinism of the so-
called superior men. These forms of dualism, detected and
attacked by Irenaeus, can be seen as derived from the
fundamental theological dualism dividing the divine or as
diverse expressions of a metaphysical dualism opposing the
world above to the world below, spirit to matter.[33]

It may be surprising that the focus of Irenaeus's
charge against the Gnostics is their dualistic outlook. It
is not my intention to decide whether Irenaeus understood

---

[31]See Sagnard, Gnose valentinienne, p. 506 and passim.
Contrary to the Clement of Str. VI and VII (e.g. Str. VII.2
and 16) and to Origen (In Jo. II.3.27-31; In Matth. 12.30)
Irenaeus does not see room in the church for classes,
distinctions, and levels due to degrees of perfection and
understanding.

[32]See Brox, Offenbarung, p. 178.

[33]Reynders ('Polémique, p. 27) says concerning the
hardening of gnostic dualism in Irenaeus's description of
it: 'Aurait-il été si difficile de rapprocher les points
de vue en transportant, par exemple, le dualisme du champ
de la métaphysique à celui de la psychologie?'. But
Irenaeus has not completely neglected to do so and to
reduce gnostic speculations to exercises in thought: see
II.12.2; II.13.1-10.

Gnosis from within,[34] faithfully grasped the gnostic self-understanding,[35] or was fair to their profound concerns.[36] The fact is that in describing the mitigated dualism which is Gnosticism[37] Irenaeus perceived two essential aspects of its dynamic system: first, its emanationist scheme expressed in the doctrine of aeons and, secondly, its dualistic outlook. He describes both aspects, relying on gnostic sources (I.praef.2).[38] But when he attacks their system, the second aspect comes to the fore almost exclusively. Why is it so? In order to account for this concentration on dualism we shall have to look at Irenaeus's non-theological motives for rejecting gnostic claims.

---

[34]See Widmann ('Irenäus', p. 171) for a negative verdict.

[35]For important elements of that self-understanding see Brox, Offenbarung, passim.

[36]F. Wisse, 'The Nag Hammadi Library and the Heresiologists', VC 25, 1971, pp. 205-23, thinks that Irenaeus did the Gnostics an injustice in considering their discourse and writings from the point of view of doctrine, while they propound rather a sort of 'mystical poetry' (p. 222). Further, Irenaeus would have too readily assumed that unity in doctrine is the only kind of unity. 'By taking the differences in mythological detail as doctrinal differences, Gnosticism came to look like an absurdly fragmented movement' (p. 221). Also K. Rudolph (Gnosis, p. 16) says concerning Irenaeus's knowledge of the Gnostics: 'Sein Wissen [ist] sehr begrenzt und einseitig gewesen'.

[37]Mitigated dualism is opposed to absolute dualism, which is more static and leads to withdrawal from the world; the latter is found in Manichaeism, but is marginal in Gnosticism. The medieval Cathars will have both forms of dualism--mitigated and absolute. See C. Thouzellier, ed., Le livre des deux principes (SC 198), Paris 1973; C. Thouzellier, Catharisme et valdéisme au Languedoc, Paris 1969.

[38]See F. Wisse, 'The Nag Hammadi Library', pp. 212-19.

3. Socio-political Motives

There are a number of incidental remarks found among
Irenaeus's arguments which cannot be considered as having
philosophical or theological character. These constitute
arguments of a third kind. In some passages they are
mentioned almost casually; in others, they are only
implicit in Irenaeus's refutation. Never are they treated
extensively as a theme. But their presence is
significant.

Because of the opposing temperaments of Irenaeus and
the Gnostics,[39] we do not expect Irenaeus to present
arguments that are exclusively intellectual. And indeed
Irenaeus's refutation reflects the suspicion harbored by
simple Christians of a theological speculation that seemed
to endanger such basic truths as the unity of God.
Irenaeus imagines himself as the spokesman of the masses,
strongly anchored in the tradition and in the faith of the
average Christian. Thus he reflects and propounds a form
of 'popular theology'[40] and is suspicious of those

---

[39]'Deux tempéraments incompatibles...' (Reynders, Polémique', p.   27).   See T.   A. Audet, 'Orientations
théologiques chez saint Irénée', Traditio 1, 1943, pp. 15-
54, who speaks of a spontaneous rather than an intellectual
reaction to Gnosticism (pp. 33-39).

[40]We take the problematic concept of 'popular
theology' to mean here the faith of the simple Christians
as opposed to the speculations of the learned. Thus also
Reynders, 'Polémique', p. 22:   'On trouvera sans doute
qu'Irénée, soucieux de sauver les simples et les doux, a un
peu négligé les meneurs'. On 'popular theology', see H. J.
Carpenter, 'Popular Christianity'. Carpenter tends to find
in the Apostolic Fathers themselves 'the bulk of popular
Christianity throughout the second century and well on into
the third' (p. 296).   It is regrettable, though, that
'popular' is here left so loosely defined and only seems to
mean the 'majority view'.   For Carpenter, popular
Christianity is characterized by its interest in morals,
discipline, and worship (see p. 300 and passim). On the
question of popular faith and learned theology in the early
centuries, see: J. Lebreton, 'Le désaccord de la foi
populaire et de la théologie savante dans l'Église
chrétienne du IIIe siècle', RHE 19, 1923, pp. 481-506; 20,

'learned' theologicans, the Gnostics, with their dangerous science and eloquence,[41] who in his eyes are mere philosophers, and bad ones at that. His natural propensity for unity and unanimity is shocked by their undisciplined discourse and behavior; they endanger the welfare of individuals as well as of the Empire.[42]

This concern for peace and unity had already been expressed in Irenaeus's intervention against rigorist and encratite tendencies that could divide the church; Irenaeus sided with those who favoured tolerance and indulgence for the lapsi.[43] It is possible that he even defended the Montanists[44] and he was inclined to show them tolerance.

1924, pp. 5-37, for whom also popular faith means the faith of the simple. He notes 'parfois opposition, plus souvent un désaccord ou du moins un malentendu entre la spéculation des savants et la foi des simples' (p. 481). See also J. Lebreton, 'Le désaccord entre la foi populaire et la théologie savante' in Fliche-Martin, Histoire de l'Église 2, Paris 1948, pp. 361-374. Looking ahead to the upcoming evolution, it could be argued that the line of development will go from 'faith of the simple' to 'common faith' (faith of the masses) to orthodoxy. Further on simple faith and theology, see N. Brox, 'Der einfache Glaube und die Theologie. Zur altkirchlichen Geschichte eines Dauer-problems', Kairos 14, 1972, pp. 161-187, esp. 167-168 on Irenaeus; A Momigliano, 'Popular Religious Beliefs and the Late Roman Historians', Studies in Church History, eds. G. J. Cuming and D. Baker, vol. 8, 1972, pp. 1-18.

[41]For a typical statement of this suspicion, see Adv. haer. II.26.1.

[42]See in this context A.H.M. Jones, 'Were Ancient Heresies National or Social Movements in Disguise?', JTS 10, 1959, pp. 280-298. In the later Roman Empire 'the generality of people firmly believed that not only individual salvation but the fortune of the empire depended on correct doctrine' (p. 296).

[43]See Eusebius, HE V.1-2; 11-18. On this controversy and Irenaeus's part in it, see P. Nautin, Lettres et écrivains chrétiens des IIe et IIIe siècles, Paris, 1961, pp. 33-61.

[44]Eusebius, HE V.4.1-2. See N. Brox, 'Juden und Heiden bei Irenäus', MTZ 16, 1965, pp. 89-106, esp. 105. See the "Excursus" below, pp. 34-40.

He was ready to praise the Empire for favoring unity and
was not interested in attacking the 'pagans'; such an
attack lies beyond his scope and could only have
contributed to jeopardizing the peace of society. In fact
he showed himself to be much harder on the Gnostics than on
the Jews and was altogether gentle with the pagans.[45] Why?
Does the proximity of the Gnostics alone account for their
passionate rejection?

Before writing against the Gnostics, Irenaeus enjoyed
the reputation of a peace-maker, tolerant and permissive.
(It is significant that 'orthodoxy' generally emerged among
those groups that favoured indulgence and opposed
rigorism.) But his permissiveness went only so far. Where
unity was seen as already broken, where authority was
challenged, Irenaeus reacted strongly. Montanists might
have represented the same threat as the Gnostics; but they
were far from Gaul. Irenaeus witnessed gnostic preaching
and perceived it as a divisive element in the Christian
communities which endangered the mission of the Church.
Irenaeus complains indeed that those who corrupt the truth
'affect the preaching of the church' (I.27.4). Concerned
with the image of the church, he thinks that they bring
dishonor upon it (I.25.3). Celsus had just (ca. 178) shown
that it was possible to take gnostic extravagances as
typically Christian.[46] The folly of the Gnostics could
draw the attention of the civil authorities. 'Men hearing
the things which they speak, and imagining that we are all
such as they, may turn away their ears from the preaching
of the truth; or, again, seeing the things they practice,
may defame us all, who have in fact no fellowship with
them, either in doctrine or in morals, or in our daily

---

[45]See Brox, 'Juden und Heiden': 'Die Juden sind
antignostisches Argument' (p. 96 n. 15a). 'Irenäus kennt
die Heiden nur friedlich...' (p. 104).

[46]See Ullmann, 'Gnostische und politische Häresie',
pp. 153-56. According to Ullmann, 'gerade die gnostische
Haltung gegenüber Welt und Menschheit ist es, die er
[Celsus] als die typisch christliche ansieht' (p. 155).

conduct' (I.25.3). Clearly the reputation of the Church is
at stake.[47] It is imperative to stress that the Christians
have nothing to do with these 'magicians' (see II.31.1-3)
and instruments of Satan. Likewise, it is essential that
Christians dissociate themselves from those radicals who
hold 'unauthorized assemblies' (III.3.2) and pour contempt
upon the martyrs (III.18.5; IV.26.3; IV.33.9) at a time
when the church needs to offer a common front to a society
still suspicious and not quite ready to welcome Christians
as reliable social partners.[48]

Irenaeus sees that, in addition to unity in its own
ranks, the authority of the church is challenged. This
makes Irenaeus especially concerned and urges him to
formulate a long series of complaints to that effect.[49]
Gnostics relativize the authority of the presbyters
(V.20.2: 'Those...who desert the preaching of the church,
call in question the knowledge of the holy presbyters, not

---

[47]In this context one might look at orthodoxy in terms
of 'ecclesiastical vested interest'. For a survey of this
question, see R. A. Markus, 'Christianity and Dissent in
Roman North Africa: Changing Perspectives in Recent Work',
Studies in Church History, ed. D. Baker, Vol. 9, 1972, pp.
21-36.

[48]To be sure, Gnostics are generally seen by Irenaeus
as Christians, since he calls them to repentance and
conversion. He does not consider them to be clearly
outside the church. At least they are close enough to the
church as to represent a threat. He himself is so close to
them that he cannot, for instance, say (as Tertullian will
do in Adv. Val. IV.1-3) that Valentinus was an intelligent
person, without feeling that he would be conceding too
much.

[49]Carpenter ('Popular Christianity', p. 297) thinks
that Irenaeus writes against the Gnostics at a time when
they had already been overcome: i.e. when the 'masses' had
already rejected them. Is that so? It seems that the
teachings of the Gnostics are of concern to Irenaeus
precisely because they teach 'inside'. Were they to teach
'outside', as Cyprian said concerning Novatian, Irenaeus
should not be curious about what they say. See S. L.
Greenslade, 'Heresy and Schism in the Later Roman Empire',
Studies in Church History 9, 1972, p. 8; N. Brox,
Offenbarung, p. 22.

taking into consideration of how much greater consequence
is a simple but religious man, than a blasphemous and
impudent sophist');[50] they criticize the Church's
understanding of Jesus.[51]   Authorities in the Church,
Gnostics insinuate, are mere servants of the demiurge;[52]
thus these authorities share in the demiurge's ambiguous
nature and have no power over the 'children of the Father'.
Scripture and tradition are freely accommodated and
misused. Gnostics criticize what the whole Church holds as
sacred (I.10.2).   They clash with all authorities and
undermine them. 'They affirm that many of his disciples'
were mistaken about Jesus (I.30.13).[53] If one adds to this
their understanding of revelation as a direct communication
made to men, instead of seeing God's revelation in his
historical deeds,[54] it might be said that they reject all
forms of mediation. As N. Brox says,[55] for the Gnostics

> Geschichte ist Unheilsgeschichte, niemals
> Heilsgeschichte, denn sie ist ja das Markmal
> der demiurgischen Welt, welche mit Gnosis
> und Heil nichts zu tun hat...[Der Gnostiker]
> kennt ausschliesslich den vertikalen
> Einbruch jenseitiger Offenbarung. Die
> Gnosis erreicht ihn im Augenblick und ohne
> Vermittlung wirklicher geschichtlicher
> Überlieferung oder Autorität.

---

[50]See Brox, Offenbarung, p. 119.

[51]See Brox, Offenbarung, p. 122.

[52]See E. H. Pagels, '"The Demiurge and His Archons"--A
Gnostic View of the Bishop and Presbyters?', HTR 69, 1976,
pp. 301-24, esp. 315-16, 319-20.

[53]See Brox, 'Antignostische', pp. 273-75; id.,
Offenbarung, p. 122.

[54]See N. Brox, 'Offenbarung--gnostisch und
christlich', Stimmen der Zeit 182, 1968, pp. 105-17, here
109-11.

[55]Brox, 'Offenbarung', pp. 110-11. See also R. A.
Markus, 'Pleroma', pp. 219-24.

Irenaeus seems to have been very impressed by the disruptive attitude of the Gnostics in his entourage and in particular to have perceived the undisciplined and revolutionary character of their outlook. This outlook is rooted in a 'Revolte gegen Zeit, Geschichte und Welt...Sie ist Negation des Vorhandenen und in Geltung Stehenden';[56] it has revolutionary contours. To him Gnostics show radical tendencies.

Without taking sides on the issue of whether ancient heresies were disguised social movements,[57] it has to be acknowledged (and Irenaeus saw it) that Gnosticism had a strong revolutionary impetus.[58] I want therefore to

---

[56]Brox, 'Antignostische', p. 277. See H.-Ch. Puech, 'La gnose et le temps', Eranos-Jahrbuch 20, 1951, pp. 57-113 (now in En quête de la gnose, 2 vols., Paris 1978); K. Rudolph, Gnosis, pp. 72, 281-90, 310. According to Rudolph the gnostic movement 'enthält eine Kritik an allem Bestehenden, die in der Antike kaum ihres gleichen findet' (p. 281). Rudolph strongly emphasizes the 'gesellschafskritische und sozialkritische Haltung der Gnosis', its 'Ablehnung der diesseitigen Herrschaftsverhältnisse'; and he see gnosis as 'sozialer Protest' (p. 310). Again, K.-W. Tröger, in Actes du Colloque international sur les textes de Nag Hammadi d'août 1978 (ed. B. Barc), (forthcoming), develops a view close to Rudolph's. The gnostic religion, as it appears in the Nag Hammadi texts, directed its protest not only against the established Church, but more specifically against the Church's assertive view of the Old Testament as well as against the this-worldliness of the Jewish tradition.

[57]See W.H.C. Frend, 'Heresy and Schism as Social and National Movements', Studies in Church History 9, 1972, pp. 37-56. A.H.M. Jones ('Popular', p. 295) writes about later heresies: 'Modern historians are retrojecting into the past the sentiments of the present age when they argue that mere religious or doctrinal dissension cannot have generated such violent and enduring animosity as that evinced by the Donatists, Arians, or Monophysites, and that the real moving force behind these movements must have been national or class feeling'. Granted; but it would be unwise to exclude a priori the impact of non-theological or non-religious factors in the emergence of the main stream in the Church. Moreover, the Gnostics' doctrines obviously had practical and political implications which were perceived by their opponents.

[58]Rudolph (Gnosis, p. 287) speaks of 'Sprengkraft'.

suggest that Irenaeus perceived the gnostic movement as
socially subversive in addition, of course, to being
theologically so. Celsus on the other hand, who saw the
whole church as a social danger, only extended to it the
accusation that Irenaeus reserved for the Gnostics.

Why then did Irenaeus attack almost exclusively the
dualistic aspect of Gnosticism? He says little against its
emanationist scheme, which he also describes. The
emanation principle is not seen as socially subversive; it
is only said to be arbitrary and absurd. But the dualist
outlook represents a social threat. It spares no mundane
authority, criticizes what is universally received, and
challenges the status quo. Its potential for disturbing
peace and order knows no limit and, consequently, Gnostics
are seen as dangerous radicals.[59]

Since Irenaeus saw the greatest threat in the
dualistic aspect of Gnosticism, he decided to concentrate
his attack upon that. It might be that the dualist
tradition contains subversive elements[60] in the same way
that 'learned theology' is often suspected by 'simple

---

[59]We can here recall the inspiring statement found in
E. Peterson, Monotheismus, pp. 104-5 n. 16: 'Die
politischen Folgen eines gnostischen oder dualistischen
Weltbildes sind m.E. noch niemals in einem grösseren
Zusammenhang dargestellt worden'. We do not pretend to
carry out the task indicated by Peterson. But it seems
appropriate to repeat here his invitation which should be
seen as a complement to the repeated calls for the study of
the sociology of gnosticism. See H. A. Green, 'Gnosis and
Gnosticism. A Study in Methodology', Numen 24, 1977, pp.
95-134.

[60]See H. Jonas, 'A Retrospective View', Proceedings of
the International Colloquium on Gnosticism, Stockholm
August 20-25, 1973, Stockholm 1977, p. 14: 'Gnosticism has
been the most radical embodiment of dualism ever to have
appeared on the stage of history...It is a split between
self and world, men's alienation from nature, the
metaphysical devaluation of nature, the cosmic solitude of
the spirit and the nihilism of mundane norms; and in its
general extremist style it shows what radicalism really
is'. The medieval Cathars can throw some light on the
subversive aspect of the dualist tradition. They too were
strongly critical of the visible church and anticlerical;

believers' of overthrowing the faith.[61] In focusing his
attack almost exclusively on one aspect of Gnosticism,
Irenaeus neglected elements that are essential to gnostic
self-understanding.   He might have seen in dualistic
teachings social and political implications that were
abhorrent to him. These non-theological factors might well
have given him the ultimate motivation for writing his
refutation.

Irenaeus thought he was in a better position to answer
the gnostic threat than his predecessors were (see
IV.praef.2). We can understand that his predecessors had
not succeeded in having the Gnostics condemned and
expelled. It is not certain that Irenaeus himself achieved
such a final overthrow. But he surely reinforced the
polarization between the two groups that were already at
odds.[62]

---

they resisted the structures of the church, especially the
Gregorian structures. See C. Thouzellier and E. Delaruelle
in Hérésies et sociétés dans l'Europe préindustrielle 11-
18e siècle (ed. J. Le Goff), Paris/La Haye 1968, pp. 111
and 153.

[61]The tension between simple believers and learned
theologians only reflects the tension, recurrent throughout
the history of theology, between Amt and learned theology.
This is not to say, however, that the masses had no share
in the gnostic movement. See N. Brox, 'Antignostische', p.
289, n. 69.

[62]It has long been fashionable to say that the impact
of the conservative Irenaeus is limited to the West. It is
attested that even the Middle Ages generally ignored Adv.
haer. (perhaps because of the no longer acceptable
eschatological section in Book V); Augustine quotes Adv.
haer. only a few times (see SC 152, pp. 46-8). But there
are now indications that Adv. haer. was known, quite early,
in Egypt. Papyrus Oxyr. 405, identified early in this
century as being a section of Adv. haer. III.9.2-3,
indicates its presence in Upper Egypt at the end of the
second or the beginning of the third century. This leads
Doutreleau to state: 'L'oeuvre d'Irénée...serait ainsi
parvenue...à plus de 400 kilometres au sud d'Alexandrie,
quelques vingt ans, et peut-être plus rapidement encore,
après sa rédaction à Lyon' (SC 210, p. 128). Many passages
of Clement's Str. are strikingly parallel to Adv. haer:
Str. II.72-75 (Stählin); III.216-7; VI.503.10-17; VII.18.

In trying to determine Irenaeus's motives and reasons
for attacking the Gnostics, I do not mean to de-emphasize
Irenaeus's theological reasoning. Nor do I intend to
question the value of his theological contribution. I am
rather interested in finding out what decided Irenaeus to
oppose the Gnostics in the way he did. I think that his
temperament accounts for part of his decision. The
subversive character of Gnosis represented an instance that
he could not see reconciled with the life in the Church.[63]
Irenaeus appears to have thought that Gnosis was aiming at
destroying all that the apostolic tradition had transmitted
and that constituted the foundation of the church. His
attack was against a life-enemy.

Irenaeus thus contributed to the formation of battle-
lines. After him, the Christian community did not step
beyond the point he fixed. Dualist ideologies have
consistently have been combatted throughout the centuries,
although they never completely disappeared. In the 12th
century gnostic dualism was still the chief enemy of the
Church,[64] important not in numbers (Cathars and Bogomils
were only small minorities), but for the threat it
represented to an institution based on the principle of
authority.

Origen himself would have known Adv. haer. if one accepts
A. Le Boulluec's hypothesis in 'Y a-t-il des traces de la
polémique anti-gnostique d'Irénée dans le Peri Archon
d'Origène?', Gnosis and Gnosticism (ed. M. Krause), Leiden
1977, pp. 138-47. See K. Koschorke, Die Polemik der
Gnostiker gegen das kirchliche Christentum, Leiden 1978, p.
247 n. 15.

[63]N. Brox (Offenbarung, pp. 33-5) points to the
'versöhnliche Haltung' of the Gnostics who did not see
their Gnosis as directly contradicting the church. 'Sie
wollen nicht ausserhalb als Häretiker, sondern in der
Kirche als Pneumatiker gelten' (p. 34). But Irenaeus
refuses all compromise with them and insists on seeing in
gnostic groups heretical 'Konventikel' ('unauthorized
assemblies' or rival communities: see SC 210, pp. 223-36
on Adv. haer. III.4.2). In that way he helped to force
them out of the community.

[64]See J. Duchesne-Guillemin, 'Dualismus', RAC 4,
Stuttgart 1959, col. 349.

Irenaeus's contribution to the exclusion of the Gnostics surely deprived the church of colorful tendencies. Theologians were told to avoid dangerous speculations and to bow before authority and the majority. But this rejection also meant that gnostic anticosmism and antisomatism[65] were said to be irreconcilable with the Christian view of salvation. It meant further that discrimination among men was attacked in favor of equality of all before God's universal plan of salvation. Such assertions certainly struck a responsive chord among the simple believers who constituted the majority. In retrospect, the fact that Irenaeus came forward at this time and in the way he did helped Christianity save its identity in the Greco-Roman melting pot.[66] That in turn prevented Christianity from being a marginal movement in the Western world.[67]

But with the triumph of Irenaeus's ideas in Rome and of the Roman theology in the fourth century, a conservative impetus was to make itself felt. Irenaeus's part in the rejection of gnosis in favor of pistis contributed to the choice of an authoritarian structure in Christianity. An authoritarian pattern was devised to meet heretical challenges,[68] the essential features of this pattern being the criterion of antiquity (apostolicity) and that of consent (majority). This pattern was to be the obligato for centuries of Christian development, while Irenaeus's style became a standard element in Christian polemic for centuries.

---

[65]'...dann ist an der gnostischen Beschimpfung der Welt und ihrer Apostrophierung als "Illusion, Schein, Nichts" sowie an den Protesten des Plotin der entscheidende Unterschied (mit Neuplatonismus) abzulesen'. N. Brox, 'Antignostische', p. 280 n. 42.

[66]See W. Bauer, Orthodoxy and Heresy in Earliest Christianity, London/Philadelphia 1972/1971, p. 240.

[67]See K. Rudolph, Gnosis, p. 391.

[68]See S. L. Greenslade, 'Heresy and Schism', pp. 1-20.

Excursus: Irenaeus and the Montanists

     Since Irenaeus is eager to protect the faith from any
deviation, his silence concerning Montanism is surprising.
He voices no clear objection against the 'new prophecy'[1]
that originated in his own Asia Minor in 156/7 (according
to Epiphanius[2]) or 172/3 (according to Eusebius[3]); and he
does not even provide us with any information on the
movement. Could it be that he agrees with Montanist views
or that he is ready to show tolerance towards those
involved in the movement? Do we find elements of an answer
in recent studies of Montanism?

     It would be relatively easy to explain Irenaeus's
silence if we were to follow F.C. Baur's view of an anti-
gnostic character of Montanism. According to Baur the
conflict between the 'Jewish' (Petrine) and the
'Hellenistic' (Pauline) versions of Christianity was to
result into a final synthesis in early Catholicism. On
this view, Montanism would clearly find its place along the
Jewish line over against the Hellenistic Gnosis and thus be
on Irenaeus's side. Such a picture of Montanism as a
counter-movement to Gnosticism has prevailed until

---

     [1]Adv.haer. IV.33.6-7 may have been directed against
Montanism, but no explicit mention of it is made.

     [2]J.A. Fischer, 'Die antimontanistischen Synoden des
2./3. Jahrhunderts' AHC 6, 1974, pp. 241-273, favors the
earlier date: 'Man darf daher vermuten, dass der
Montanismus um 157 auftrat und die Bewegung des
Urmontanismus mit den 70er Jahren ihren Höhepunkt
erreichte, was zu ihrer Trennung von der Grosskirche
führte' (p. 247). The same position is found in Elsa
Gibson, 'Montanism and its Monuments', Diss. Harvard
University 1974.

     [3]The later date is preferred by D. Powell,
'Tertullianists and Cataphrygians', VC 29, 1975, pp. 33-54,
esp. p. 41; and by T.D. Barnes, 'The Chronology of
Montanism', JTS NS 21, 1970, pp. 403-408.

recently, taking its cue from the Montanist Tertullian who did fight the Gnostics.

K. Froehlich[4] has taken a radically different approach. Questioning this 'antithetical picture' as inspired ultimately by a Hegelian scheme, he has shown, on the basis of the Montanist oracles, how much Montanism and Gnosticism have in common. He pointed to the striking 'closeness of terminology and thought' (p. 108) in the two movements and concluded that there is 'a common matrix ... in which Jewish elements played a major part' (pp. 109-111). If one accepts Froehlich's extreme view of the proximity of the two movements, it becomes most difficult to explain Irenaeus's silence on Montanism.

Is the local proximity of the Gnostics to Irenaeus sufficient to account for his passionate rejection of them? He would not have been concerned with a movement so geographically remote from Gaul as Montanism was. But this view encounters difficulties. Irenaeus did not limit his doctrinal worries to the Rhone valley; although he was primarily concerned with local heretics, he did attack gnostic groups all around the Mediterranean and the geographical factor counts for little in a refutation of all heresies. Further, we cannot have Irenaeus plead ignorance. If it is granted that the Montanist movement was making its strongest impact between 156 and 172[5], it would be difficult to see how Irenaeus could have ignored it unless he had already left Asia Minor at that time (he was in Rome under Anicetus, who was bishop there from 154 on). But even if it were granted that he had not known of the Montanist movement while in Asia Minor, how could Irenaeus have totally ignored the crisis that was echoed in

---

[4]K. Froehlich, 'Montanism and Gnosis', in The Heritage of the Early Church. Essays in Honor of the Very Reverend G.V. Florovsky, eds. D. Neiman and M. Schatkin, Roma 1973, pp. 91-111.

[5]See Th. Baumeister, 'Montanismus und Gnostizismus', TrTZ 87, 1978, pp. 44-60, here pp. 49-50.

Lyons itself a few years before he undertook the writing of
Adv.haer.[6] as witnessed by the letter he wrote[7] to the
churches in Asia and Phrygia on behalf of the confessors
and the brethren in the Rhone valley (Eusebius, HE V. 1-
4)? It should be kept in mind, however, that the explicit
issue that occasioned Irenaeus's letter had to do with the
lapsi and the attitude to take toward them (Irenaeus
favored indulgence), and that this letter does not prove
that Montanism as such had entered the Rhone country; it
only proves that the events taking place in Asia Minor were
known to the churches of Vienne and Lyons.[8]

     If the geographical factor alone cannot account for
Irenaeus's silence, can the chronology be of some avail?
The anti-Montanist literature was written during the last
quarter of the second century and the first decade of the
third[9]. This obviously leaves Montanism, at least early
Montanism, contemporary to Irenaeus who cannot be provided
here with an alibi. At the time he was writing his
refutation of the Gnostics, he must have been aware that

---

[6]J.A. Fischer, 'Die antimontanistichen', p. 247:
'Schon um 177/178 bezeugen die gallischen Gemeinden von
Lyon und Vienne Kenntnis der "neuen Prophetie"'.

[7]Irenaeus himself wrote the letter, according to P.
Nautin, Lettres et écrivains chrétiens des IIe et IIIe
siècles, Paris 1961, pp. 54-61.

[8]Nautin, Lettres, p. 100 writes concerning the
information that prompted the letter of the churches of
Vienne and Lyons: 'La lettre que l'évêque d'Éphese lui
[=Irénée] avait écrite signalait que les adversaires
asiates de l'indulgence se réclamaient, en plus du titre de
'martyrs', de révélations charismatiques. Il est croyable
que c'étaient celles de Montan, de Priscilla et de
Maximilla; mais le nom des prophètes n'est pas donné'. See
also pp. 39-43.

[9]F. Blanchetière, 'Le montanisme originel I', RevSR
52, 1978, pp. 118-134, here p. 132; Th. Baumeister,
'Montanismus', p. 52. J.A. Fischer, 'Die
antimontanistischen', p. 257, holds that the first
antimontanist synods (not identical with the earliest
antimontanist literature) met around 200.

others were engaged in debating about Montanism[10]. Did he
wish to leave it to others to speak against the
Montanists?

We must look more closely at the nature of the
Montanist movement itself if we want to understand why
Irenaeus remained silent. There is wide agreement today on
the nature of the movement: continuing or reviving early
Christian prophetism, Montanist prophecy centered around
the intense belief in the proximity of the end of the
world. The accompanying eschatological exaltation resulted
in a program in which the experience of the Spirit and
moral rigorism occupied an important place[11].

Because Montanist eschatology presented features
similar to early Christian eschatology, the movement has
generally been characterized as 'conservative'[12], or as
'restorative'[13], or as 'reactionary'[14]. It has also been
declared archaic on the basis of formal similarities with
early Christian expectations. But archaizing or not, the
Montanist movement, in reviving the original expectation
and prophecy[15], was the expression of a struggle for

---

[10]F. Wisse suggests that Irenaeus's silence may be
explained by the fact that Justin's Syntagma (before 147)
or a reworking of it, which he follows, was silent about
Montanism.

[11]See K. Froehlich, 'Montanism', p. 92; Th.
Baumeister, 'Montanismus', pp. 48-50; J.A. Fischer, 'Die
antimontanistischen', pp. 241-244, 261-263: all rely on
standard presentations of Montanism in the last 100 years.

[12]C. Andresen, Die Kirchen der alten Christenheit,
Stuttgart 1971, p. 111: 'In gewisser Beziehung trägt der
Montanismus Züge eines revolutionären Konservatismus'.

[13]K. Aland, 'Bemerkungen zum Montanismus und zur
frühchristlichen Eschatologie' in Kirchengeschichtliche
Entwürfe, Gütersloh 1960, pp. 105-148: '... Versuch einer
Restauration' (p. 143).

[14]H. Paulsen, 'Die Bedeutung des Montanismus für die
Herausbildung des Kanons', VC 32, 1978, pp. 19-52, here p.
39.

[15]See F. Blanchetière, 'Le montanisme originel II',
RevSR 53, 1979, pp. 1-22, here p. 19.

identity in remote geographical areas for which the
adaptation of the church to the world in its missionary
efforts represented a serious threat[16].

Thus eschatological exaltation, dramatic experience of
the Spirit, and moral discipline seem to have characterized
the Montanist movement. There appears to be nothing in
this picture that would be a departure from the doctrine of
the church. No essential 'addition or subtraction' was
made to the beliefs held as orthodox. This is why students
of the movement have generally been led to the conclusion
that it was not its beliefs, but its eschatological
attitude expressed in charismatic and ecstatic prophecy and
in ethical rigorism which constituted the stumbling block
for the opponents of Montanism.

Since the Montanist doctrine was not perceived by
Irenaeus as objectionable[17], it is understandable that
he would have nothing to say about the movement. The
Elenchos and Epiphanius also do not find many objections
beyond some innovations in the realm of praxis (Ref.
III.19.2; Pan.haer. 48.1.4).

But not only did Irenaeus fail to discover anything
theoretically objectionable in the 'new prophecy'; there is
even a certain congeniality between the two. In both a
conservative element is at play. Irenaeus might have
shared with the Montanists, beyond differences due to the
contexts, the view that the Church's identity was
threatened by recent developments. He positively had
sympathy for the Montanist eschatological message. Book V
of Adv.haer. testifies to millenarian views that are well
in keeping with Montanist eschatology. Epideixis 99 and
Adv.haer. II.32.4. show Irenaeus's respect for prophetic
charisma. Further, if one grants the archaizing nature of

---

[16]See Th. Baumeister, 'Montanismus', pp. 52-53.

[17]See J.A. Fischer, 'Die antimontanistischen', p. 245
and note 26. It was only decades later that their doctrine
of God and of the Trinity was questioned (see pp. 263-
273).

Montanism, such a feature was not in itself a problem for
the bishop of Lyons. He had very strong feelings about the
normative character of the primitive, apostolic times, and
also agreed with Montanists on the normative validity of
the written tradition[18], although they would not admit with
him that the time of revelation was definitively over.

Irenaeus was investigating systems of thought that put
forward free interpretations of the original message of
Christianity and resulted at times in reprehensible
behavior. He was not concerned about refuting excesses in
moral rigorism resulting from a zealous interest in
orthodox faith. In its origin at least, the Montanist view
did not appear to Irenaeus as diverging in matters of
faith, or as drawing practical demands from wrong premises.
At times Irenaeus did oppose rigorism; but he saw no room
for such an opposition in a work written to refute
heresies.

Be that as it may, a riddle remains. We have assumed
that Irenaeus knew of the Montanist movement and found
nothing objectionable in it. We must now argue that he had
only a limited knowledge of the movement. Had he known it
better, it is difficult to see how he could have found
nothing objectionable in some tenets of the doctrine
itself. How could he have overlooked the challenge to
church leadership embedded in ecstatic prophecy? How could
he have approved of the tendency of Montanism, visible in
Tertullian, to further a church of the Spirit over against
a church of the bishops?[19] Was this only a later

---

[18]See H. Paulsen, 'Die Bedeutung', pp. 51-52.

[19]See Th. Baumeister, 'Montanismus', p. 50; J.A.
Fischer, 'Die antimontanistischen', pp. 262-263.   C.
Andresen, Die Kirchen, p. 115, describes the Montanists as
'radikale Kritiker allen Kirchentums'; but if this
description is correct, and given Irenaeus's ecclesiology,
it is difficult to understand how Andresen can make the
following categorical statement concerning the Montanists:
'Man fand in Irenäus einen Fürsprecher' (p. 111).
     It is the martyrs of Lyons, rather than Irenaeus, who
would be in agreement with the Montanist thesis, according

manifestation of the movement that Irenaeus could not have
observed?

to H.   Kraft, 'Die lyoner Märtyrer und der Montanismus',
Les martyrs de Lyon (177), Colloques internationaux du CNRS
(20-23 septembre 1977), Paris 1978, pp. 233-247.   Among
both groups, Kraft speculates, we observe the same
ecclesiological vision and the same emphasis on the
superiority of charismatic ministry against institutional
ministry.   He says concerning the martyrs: 'Sie [waren]
dem institutionellen Amt gegenüber zurückhaltend' (p. 239).
However, Kraft concludes (p. 243) 'dass wir die Lyoner
trotz ihrer Anerkennung der montanistischen Prophetie,
trotz ihrem Enthusiasmus und trotz ihrem Eintreten für den
Montanismus doch nicht als Montanisten ansehen können'.

II. THE ELENCHOS AGAINST ALL HERESIES

The study of the arguments put forward against the
Gnostics in the Elenchos[1], as any study of the Elenchos, is
inevitably bound to the riddle associated with the name
'Hippolytus'. Everything concerning Hippolytus has indeed
become enigmatic. Since we wish to deal here with the
Elenchos to the exclusion of any other work attributed to
Hippolytus, a brief consideration of some of the problems
connected with the authorship and scope of the Elenchos
should be enough to justify such a limitation.

Who was the author of the Elenchos? The work was
discovered in 1842 and published in 1851. Soon Jacobi,
Duncker, Bunsen, and others were to suggest Hippolytus as
the author, in spite of a first attribution to Origen
(Origen was proposed because of references to him in the
margins of the manuscript; Migne still has the Elenchos at
the end of Origen's works[2].) Jacobi's suggestion was

---

[1]The work is referred to in the following ways:
Elenchos, taken from the title of each of the ten Books
(τοῦ κατὰ πασῶν αἱρέσεων ἐλέγχου βίβλος...); Refutatio
omnium haeresium (abbreviated Ref., which is generally
used); Philosophumena, which strictly applies only to the
first four Books (see Ref. IV. 51.14; IX.8.2.). The
critical edition is by P. Wendland, Hippolytus Werke III.
Refutatio omnium haeresium. GCS 26, Leipzig 1916. English
translation by J.H. Macmahon, ANF, vol. 5, and better, by
F. Legge Philosophumena, 2 vols., London 1921. French
translation (almost complete) with introduction and notes
by A. Siouville, Hippolyte de Rome. Philosophumena ou
réfutation de toutes les hérésies, 2 vols., Paris 1928.
German translation by K. Preysing in BKV[2]. Rh. 1, Bd. 40,
München 1922. - References are given here to Wendland's
edition. Our translation takes account of the above-
mentioned translations into modern languages.

[2]PG 16 ter. The story of the attribution of the
Elenchos is recounted by G. Ficker, Studien zur
Hippolytfrage, Leipzig 1893, where references are found.
See also Wendland in GCS 26, p. xxiii, and Legge,
Philosophoumena I, ff.5.8.

accepted by the majority of the historians of ancient Christian literature. But the riddle has other dimensions. Who was represented on the statue of a teacher found in 1551 on the Via Tiburtina and since 1959 placed in the Vatican Library? In general it is said to be the statue of Hippolytus, antipope as well as father of the church and martyr. Was Hippolytus the author of the many writings mentioned on the sides of the statue or reported by later writers from Eusebius to Photius? Despite the diverse character of these writings, he is generally agreed to be their author.

Since 1947 P. Nautin has faced anew the problems surrounding Hippolytus. He has come up with a thesis that has been accepted by only a few historians of Christian literature in the first centuries.[3] On the basis of a comparative analysis of the language and thought of various writings attributed to Hippolytus (especially of the Elenchos and the Fragment against Noëtus, taking the latter as surely written by Hippolytus), he distinguishes two authors[4] representing two very different types of mind and

---

[3]From his Hippolyte et Josipe. Contribution à l'histoire de la littérature chrétienne du troisième siècle, Paris 1947, through many other studies up to his contribution to Aufstieg und Niedergang der römischen Welt (Hg. H. Temporini und W. Haase), Berlin/New York (forthcoming), P. Nautin has not modified his thesis in any significant way; rather he has substantiated it further. For a survey of the debate about Nautin's thesis, see R. Butterworth, Hippolytus of Rome: Contra Noëtum, Heythrop Monographs 2, London 1977, pp. 21-33, where the debate is referred to in the context of a new look at the so-called Fragment against Noëtus. - Incidentally, Butterworth's analysis of the structure of Contra Noëtum leads him to the conclusion that it 'is no concluding fragment of an otherwise lost work'. It 'stands well on its own' (p. 117). Formally, the work 'appears to be an outstanding ... example of the Christian adaptation of profane diatribe for anti-heretical and teaching purposes' (p. 141). - See also M. Richard, 'Bibliographie de la controverse', PO 27, 1954, pp. 271-272.

[4]R.A. Lipsius, Die Quellen der ältesten Ketzergeschichte neu untersucht, Leipzig 1875, pp. 117 ff.

between whom the writings we know must be respectively divided: Josipos and Hippolytus. Josipos was a member of the Roman clergy, who became antipope when Callistus was elected[5] and founded a schismatic community; it is his statue that was discovered on the Via Tiburtina; he died after 235 and was the pretentious and superficial author of the Elenchos, of the Synagoge, of a De Universo, etc. Hippolytus lived in Palestine or in a nearby province and wrote between 222 and 250; he was the author, traditional by character, of a Syntagma against all heresies, of which we possess the final part only, known as the Fragment against Noëtus (this identification of the Fragment as being the final section of the Syntagma is, however, questioned by many scholars), subsequent to the Elenchos (here Nautin departs from the common opinion based on Ref. I. prooem. 1), of which it is but a reworking; of a Commentary on Daniel, of the Apostolic Tradition, etc. This Hippolytus was soon identified with an homonymous Roman martyr.

Nautin's thesis had the merit of introducing some plausibility into the problem of authorship[6]. But it was

---

and passim, also saw many difficulties in identifying the author of the Elenchos with Hippolytus. See already his Zur Quellenkritik des Epiphanius, Wien 1865, pp. 70 and 26, n. 3, where an identification is said to be only 'wahrscheinlich' and the name 'Pseudorigenes' is still preferred. However, for Harnack, Zur Quellenkritik des Gnosticismus, Leipzig 1873, pp. 170 ff, the identification of the author as being Hippolytus was 'zweifellos sicher'. Finally, A. Hilgenfeld, Die Ketzergeschichte des Urchristentums, Leipzig 1884, passim, quite wisely, we think, makes a consistant distinction between Hippolytus I and Hippolytus II, the latter being the author of the Elenchos.

[5]The Elenchos attacks Callistus mostly for his tendency toward modalism and his softening of church discipline, and only secondarily for presumed political ambitions (see Ref.IX. 11-12).

[6]The controversy around Nautin's work has been at times violent. Many critiques, among them M. Richard's, were thought to have administered 'den schlagenden Beweis'

generally rejected without any new alternative being
offered to solve the 'apories' he had pointed to. Recent
authors have continued to regard Hippolytus as the author
of the Elenchos. Until fresh studies of the problem are
made we shall find ourselves unfortunately bound to do the
same and shall refrain from placing a question mark by the
name of Hippolytus every time we refer to the author of the
Elenchos.

When therefore, in the following pages, we write
'Hippolytus' we mean the author of the Elenchos, and of the
Elenchos alone. We shall look at this work as a whole
without considering other related writings attributed to
Hippolytus. Our intention is to discover the character of
the arguments against the heretics proposed in the
Elenchos. But before tackling this task, we must mention
another problem that will help us determine the context of

(W. Schneemelcher, 'Notizen', ZKG 68, 1957, pp. 394-395)
against his thesis. Others could not see its usefulness
('eine weitere überflüssige Auseinandersetzung', pronounced
K. Beyschlag, 'Kallist und Hippolyt', TZ 20, 1964, pp. 103-
124, here p. 105, Anm. 11). In the aftermath of the
controversy, M. Richard was ready to make but one
concession: The Fragment against Noëtus cannot have the
same author as the Elenchos; but he added, in agreement
with some other scholars: It is the Fragment which was not
written by Hippolytus, the Elenchos was his work
('Hippolyte de Rome', DS VII, Paris 1968, cols. 531-571,
here 533). Richard concludes (ibid.): 'Le pseudo-Josipe
doit donc être éliminé de l'histoire de l'ancienne
littérature chrétienne'. However, the problems obviously
persist.
   The discussions of Hippolytus's historical and
literary identity have not yet produced any substantial
unanimity among scholars, as is shown by V. Loi, 'La
problematica storica-letteraria su Ippolito di Roma', in
Ricerche su Ippolito, Studia Ephemeridis 'Augustinianum'
13, Roma 1977, pp. 9-16. In the same volume ('L'identità
letteraria di Ippolito di Roma', pp. 67-88), Loi reviews
anew the literary witnesses and distinguishes, in a way
similar to Nautin's, two groups of works by two distinct
writers; he refuses to postulate a unique author who would
have gone through a profound psychological and cultural
evolution as some have recently done in order to explain
away the discrepancies. - In favor of Richard's position,
see recently R.M. Hübner, 'Die Hauptquelle des Epiphanius
(Pan.haer. 65) über Paulus von Samosata', ZKG 90, 1979, p.
57.

our study of anti-gnostic arguments: what was the real purpose of the Elenchos?

The goal of the Elenchos is no more obvious than the identity of its author. As the title of each of the ten Books of the Elenchos recalls (τοῦ κατὰ πασῶν αἱρέσεων ἐλέγχου βίβλος ...), Hippolytus certainly intends to refute all the heresies that are known to him[7]. But it was already proposed by d'Alès in 1906[8]--and more recently by Koschorke[9]--that Hippolytus's secret and main purpose was to confute Callistus and his group. The attack against Callistus occurs in Book IX; the previous Books would only set out the context and 'genealogy' of that personal enemy who appears as the final product of a long history of the degradation of truth. This view of the main purpose of the work can claim for itself the formal disposition of the presentation of heresies, which 'culminates' in the heresy of Callistus. Moreover, as Koschorke mentions, it was a well-known polemical technique to retroject contemporary controversies into heresies of the past. Finally, it is clear that to find a place for an enemy in a catalogue of deviants amounts to demystifying him and dissolving the magic of his reputation. Such a view of the purpose of the Elenchos, however, rests on rather weak internal indications. To be sure, Callistus was an important concern of the author of the Elenchos and for that reason

---

[7]A. Hilgenfeld, Ketzergeschichte, p. 68 saw the enterprise of the Elenchos as similar to that of Luke: 'Hippolytus II steht unter den ältesten Häresiologen ähnlich da, wie Lukas unter den synoptischen Evangelisten. Nach so manchen Vorgängern hat er es aufs Neue unternommen, allem von vorn an nachzugehen und neue Forschungen oder Erfahrungen angebracht...'.

[8]A. d'Alès, La théologie de saint Hippolyte, Paris 1906, pp. 78, 104 and 211.

[9]K. Koschorke, Hippolyts Ketzerbekämpfung und Polemik gegen die Gnostiker: Eine Tendenzkritische Untersuchung seiner 'Refutatio omnium haeresium', Wiesbaden 1975, pp. 60-73. Callistus would be 'der Zielpunkt der Polemik der Refutatio'.

he is placed in the chain of heretics three times (Ref. IX.7.1ff.; IX.3;IX.12). But the overarching idea of Book IX lies in the fact that all the heresies mentioned therein are contemporary. The unity of the Book is broken if it is said to aim at unmasking Callistus: why then would Hippolytus, after dealing with Noetus and Callistus, make such a long report on the Elchasaites and the Jews (Ref. IX.13-30, that is, more than half of the Book), which would be completely alien to his presumed goal: Callistus[10]? It appears that Callistus remains only one among many heretics whom the Elenchos wishes to unmask.

C. Andresen[11], for his part, thinks that Hippolytus's refutation would have been conceived as an answer to the challenge to Christianity represented by Celsus's Alēthēs logos. Indeed one reads in Ref. X.34.1., at the end of the 'exposition of orthodox doctrine', therefore presumably expressing the concluding word of the Elenchos: Such is the true doctrine (ἀληθὴς λόγος) about the Divine. According to Andresen, Hippolytus would have developed a 'Geschichtspolemik' apparent wherever he goes beyond his Vorlage, particularly Irenaeus, and especially where he puts forward a proof for the priority of Christianity over pagan philosophy and propounds a theory of the double depravation of truth (from philosophers to heretics, from one sect to another). But on both of these accounts Hippolytus is again following Irenaeus, as N. Brox has shown[12]. To see the Elenchos as 'Anti-Alēthēs Logos', while Hippolytus entirely lacks originality and

---

[10]Although, inventing a seemingly artificial link, Hippolytus does say that Alcibiades (a disciple of Elchasai) took occasion (Ref. IX,13) from the existence of the school of Callistus and disseminated his knavish tricks in the whole world.

[11]C. Andresen, Logos und Nomos. Die Polemik des Kelsos wider das Christentum, Berlin, 1955, pp. 387-392.

[12]N. Brox, 'Kelsos und Hippolytos. Zur frühchristlichen Geschichtspolemik', VC 20, 1966, pp. 150-158.

'geschichtstheologische[n] Hintergrund'[13], would rest on too thin a basis. Moreover, why would the Elenchos contain detailed descriptions and refutations of heresies which are utterly beyond Celsus's scope and quite indifferent to him? Again, the title of the work reminds us that its author intended a refutation of all heresies, including the gnostic heresies which are our main concern here.

The discussions just mentioned give but a slight idea of the intricate problems connected with the interpretation of the Elenchos. Some of its features, however, are clear. For instance, its formal structure: Books I-IV (II and III are missing) deal with pagan philosophy, mysteries, and astrology as being the ancestors of heresies; Books V-IX, with all heresies seen as 'plagiates' of pagan doctrines; Book X summarizes the preceding Books and expounds the orthodox doctrine. Another point is clear: Hippolytus thought he was refuting heresies. It is with the latter point that we are concerned. Without presupposing a solution to the above-mentioned problems, can we find in this work a central argument against the heretics, especially against the many types of Gnostics? In order to answer this question we must first deal with the three ways of refuting heresies that are encountered throughout the work.

1. Hippolytus's Three Ways of Refuting Heresies

Without pronouncing definitively on the validity of its thesis[14], we find in Koschorke's study of the Elenchos

---

[13]Brox, 'Kelsos', p. 157.

[14]Koschorke, Ketzerbekämpfung, pp. 4-5, where the thesis is found: 'Hippolyts Quellenwert zur Kenntnis der von ihm dargestellten gnostischen Gruppen ist sehr viel niedriger, und seine absichtliche Umgestaltung vorgegebener Nachrichten sehr viel weitreichender, als weithin angenommen wird. Vor allem fällt Hippolyt aus als Zeuge über Erscheinungsbild und Artikulationsweise der christlich-gnostischen Häresien'. See also p. 94.

a very useful clarification of Hippolytus's ways of dealing
with heretics.   Koschorke distinguishes in the Elenchos
three types of refutation, which amount to three axioms of
its author; each of these, in Koschorke's thesis,
definitely biases the content of what he reports on the
heretics, distorts the image of the Gnostics, and shows how
little Hippolytus (contrary to Irenaeus or Clement of
Alexandria) had to do with them. Starting from Koschorke's
analysis, we shall consider these three methods of
refutation.   Although they could be reduced to a unique
way, they represent three different aspects of the
argumentation found in the Elenchos and have, for that
reason, to be presented separately.   These methods
had already been used by Hippolytus's predecessors, but
less systematically.

     A.   Hippolytus's main concern is to show that the
heretics have been plagiarizing the Greeks[15].   This
affirmation recurs as a leitmotiv in the Elenchos and is
supposed to disqualify all heresies as being un-Christian.
The objective of the Elenchos is stated at the outset:

> [To show] the sources from which they drew
> their attempts; that their theories owe
> nothing to the holy scriptures, nor have
> they been concocted by holding fast to the
> tradition of any saint; but their theories
> have their source in the wisdom of the
> Greeks, in the systems of philosophers, in
> would-be mysteries, and the vagaries of
> astrologers. (Ref. I, prooem. 8)

By carrying out this program, Hippolytus will unveil the
heretics as godless (ἀθέους).

---

[15]We find a similar attempt in Tertullian, De
praescriptione haereticorum, 7 (ed. R. Refoulé, CCL 1, pp.
192-193), and only incidentally in Irenaeus (e.g. Adv.
haer. II.14.1-6).

This objective determines the plan of the Elenchos: first, to present the pagan doctrines; then to present the heresies as borrowings from them.

> It seems, therefore, advisable, first to
> expose the opinions advanced by the
> philosophers of the Greeks, and to show to
> our readers that these doctrines are of
> greater antiquity than these [heresies], and
> are more august concerning the divinity;
> then, to compare each heresy with the
> corresponding philosophical system, so as to
> show that the earliest champion of each
> heresy availed himself of the theories [of a
> philosopher], appropriated these principles,
> and, impelled from these into worse,
> constructed his own doctrine (δόγμα).
> (Ref. I, prooem. 8-9)

The whole work is expected to show the heretics as plagiatores (κλεψίλογοι : Ref. I, prooem. 11; see IV.51.14; X.34.2). It suffices, in the author's mind, to link a doctrine to philosophy or to astrology. This link throws ipso facto the greatest suspicion upon it: by confronting the heresiarch with those who first held his tenets he is shown in his miserable nakedness (see Ref. IV.46.1); he has borrowed his doctrines from the Gentiles and viciously presented them as being from God (see Ref. IX.31.1).

Hippolytus displays much learning in Books I and IV (Books II - III are no longer extant) in presenting the doctrines of the Greeks, the Indians, the Celts, astrologers, and magicians. Such a presentation, to be sure, could have a striking effect and accredit its author in the eyes of the readers. Hippolytus's knowledge in pagan matters, however, seems to be entirely second-hand. He relies for Book I on a biographical compendium and on a summary of Theophrastus's Φυσικῶν Δόξαι [16], and in Book IV

---

[16]On Hippolytus's sources in Books I-IV, see P. Wendland's introduction to GCS 26, pp. xvii-xxi, and also

he is merely transcribing large sections from Sextus
Expiricus, from a commentary on the Timaeus, etc.

Even more problematic than the affirmation of a link
between heresy and philosophy is the way Hippolytus
establishes a link between each heresy and a philosophical
doctrine or a pagan practice in his attempt to show that it
is not derived from scripture (see e.g. Ref. V.7.8:   οὐκ
ἀπὸ τῶν γραφῶν ἀλλὰ καὶ τοῦτο ἀπὸ τῶν μυστικῶν).
Most of the time this link seems artificial. For instance,
if the Naassenes teach that the serpent is the humid
element, they do so following Thales of Miletus (Ref.
V.9.13).   Basilides is said to have copied Aristotle's
teaching (Plato would have seemed to us less unlikely)
(Ref. VII.24.1-2).   Marcion would have borrowed his views
from Empedocles (Ref. VII, 29-31), a very disappointing
statement since Marcion owes so little to Greek philosophy.
Justin the Gnostic is said to depend on the Greeks,
especially on Herodotus, although his thought, from
Hippolytus's description, could just as well belong to a
Semitic milieu (Ref. V.23-28).   Is Hippolytus better
acquainted with the heretics than with their pagan
'models'? It is difficult to answer this question in a
positive way.   Although he sometimes shows more
acquaintance with pagan doctrines than Irenaeus does, what
he adds to Irenaeus concerning the Gnostics must be
received with the utmost caution since Hippolytus, in his
constant effort to force gnostic views into philosophic
systems, does not hesitate to distort them.

Hippolytus's own acknowledgment, e.g. Ref. IV.8.1. J.
Dillon, The Middle Platonists. A Study of Platonism 80
B.C. to A.D. 220, London 1977, p. 414, has a rather
positive view of Hippolytus's use of his sources; he writes
concerning the summary of Platonic doctrines in Ref. I.19:
'Hippolytus' evidence (or that of his source), brief and
sketchy as it is, nevertheless reveals a number of
interesting formulations of doctrine of which we have no
other evidence, and helps to round out our idea of what
constituted the basic course in Platonism (at least in
respect of Physics and Ethics) in the second century A.D.'

This way of establishing a relationship between heresy and philosophy might cast doubt on the Elenchos as a source of information on heretics. However, the procedure just examined shows the way in which the Elenchos deals with heretics. Thus the first feature of this method clearly emerges: the author of the Elenchos thought that a good way of refuting the heretics was to establish a link between them and the pagan thinkers in a family tree of decreasing truth. In the mind of Hippolytus, this suspect filiation creates the context within which an argument against the heretics can be launched.

B. Hippolytus's effort to show the heretics as plagiarizing from the Greeks is an essential element of his overall program: to uncover the heretical doctrines, to strip away the veil hiding their wickedness, to bring them into the full light of the day. This program itself, and its realization, constitutes the second way of refuting heresies found in the Elenchos.

Irenaeus had already stated that to expose the doctrines of the Gnostics was to refute them (Adv. haer. I.31.3). But in Adv. haer. the 'exposition' as refutation played a subordinate role; it was always clearly distinct from the argumentation. What counted for Irenaeus was the 'sachliche Auseinandersetzung' with the Gnostics and this discussion was based on reason, Bible, and theology. We witness in the Elenchos almost a complete disappearance of this type of argumentation. Even the presentation of how the heretics based their doctrines on scriptures, which, to be sure, they interpreted in a 'wicked' way, fades out. This presentation formed a lengthy preamble to Irenaeus's exegetical discussion (Adv.haer. I.1-21). But it would obviously have defeated Hippolytus's purpose: to reveal the un-Christian origin of heresy in pagan doctrines. Hippolytus is unwilling to dignify heretical views, which are only a juggling with philosophical or astrological bits (see Ref. VI.37.1; VI.52.1-2).

In Hippolytus's exposition of heretical views the
terms ἐλέγχω-ἔλεγχος are given a specific meaning. Usually
the verb means 'to prove, to disprove, to prove by a
reductio ad impossibile, to refute'. It can mean 'to
expose' only in such a context, that is, to expose with a
view to a refutation, to make a complete inventory before
the attack. In the Elenchos the meaning of 'exposition' is
prior. Such an exposition is thought to be an unmasking,
performed for the readers as well as for the Gnostics
themselves who did not know the real nature of their
doctrines and who should be amazed and even disgusted upon
discovering it. The exposition is actually the refutation
and Hippolytus can dispense with proper argumentation.

A good example of this role of the exposition is found
in the conclusion to the notice on the Peratae where
Hippolytus writes, after having repeatedly stated their
dependence upon astrology:

> I consider that I have clearly exposed the
> Peratic heresy; by many [arguments] I have
> brought out in the light the heresy which is
> always hiding itself, and mixes up
> everything to everything, and is one that
> disguises its own venom; it seems useless to
> advance any further accusation, the opinions
> propounded by [the heretics] being
> sufficient for their own condemnation.
> (Ref. V.18 emphasis added)

Four elements constitutive of Hippolytus's 'refutation' are
present here; we shall look at them more closely.

1) To refute, for Hippolytus, is to expose; more
precisely, it is to expose some tenets of a heresy and to
point to its dependence upon non-Christian sources. In the
Elenchos, this usually is accompanied by a selection of
particular elements that can be linked with pagan
doctrines. Often this amounts to a twisting; at least, the
elements presented by Hippolytus are sometimes the most
absurd or repulsive ones (see e.g. Ref. V.14. 1-10;

17,13...) by which, it is expected, the readers will be
disgusted.

2) To refute is to unveil a secret doctrine.
Hippolytus makes much of the secret character of heretical
doctrines and his program consists in breaking that secret
(see Ref.I.prooem.2-5; 8). It is hard to imagine that the
doctrines actually were secret since heretics possessed
writings that were available to the public and even to
inimical readers like Hippolytus. But more important, the
secret which Hippolytus intends to reveal resides in the
(presumably unsuspected) dependence of heretical teachings
upon pagan views, a dependence that has been revealed to us
through a problematic procedure. A typical divulging of
such a pseudo-secret is found in Ref. VII.30.1: 'When,
therefore, Marcion or some one of his hounds barks against
the Demiurge, ... we ought to say to them that ...
Empedocles announced such (tenets).' To point to Empedocles
should automatically refute Marcion.

3) This type of exposition obviates further
argumentation. The avoidance of argumentation is a
major feature of the Elenchos. At the end of an
exposition, precisely when the reader expects a discussion
of what had just been presented, he is regularly confronted
with the affirmation: ἣν ἱκανῶς ἡλέγχθαι ὑφ' ὑμῶν νομίζω .
'I think we have sufficiently exposed (refuted) this
doctrine...' (Ref. VII.31.8; see V.11; V.18; V.28' VI.37.1;
etc.). The exposition, in Hippolytus's eyes, amounts to an
argumentation and a refutation. The concluding statement
in Ref. IX.31.102 follows that format: heretics have
borrowed their doctrines from Gentiles and have then
presented them as divine teachings, as Books V to IX are
thought to have demonstrated and refuted.

4) Finally, such an exposition of heretical
doctrines constitutes by itself their denunciation. To
show how Marcion took his ideas from Empedocles

(Ref.VII.30.1) is all that the refutation is about; nothing
else is necessary, and Marcion's doctrine is thereby
utterly discredited (see the similar procedure in
Ref. V.7.8; 9.13; VI.29.1; 27.1; etc.).

Could the heretics recognize themselves in such an
exposition[17]? It is very doubtful that the image of the
Gnostics presented by Hippolytus fits the real Gnostics.
That image seems to have been concocted in Hippolytus's
study as a commodity for the polemist. But more important,
we miss here something that we found in Irenaeus: a real
attempt at gaining some insight into the gnostic
'hypothesis' through a direct encounter with them. A rare
insight of this kind is found in Ref. VII.27.11 concerning
the Basilidians:

> Their whole theory turns around the mixing
> of the universal seed, its discrimination,
> and the restoration of the mixed parts into
> their original place. (ὅλη γὰρ αὐτῶν ἡ ὑπόθεσις...
> σύνκυσις ... φυλοκρίνησις ... ἀνακατάστασις ...)

But this sort of insight plays only a limited role in the
section on the Basilidians, and no role at all in the rest
of the Elenchos. Hippolytus does not seem interested in
perceiving the 'rule' or 'hypothesis' of gnostic thought.
To do so would not have necessarily amounted to a
distortion or to a reduction of gnostic ideas into a
systematic scheme[18]; rather it would have fulfilled the
necessary hermeneutical condition of a real discussion
based on the understanding of gnostic thought-processes and
vision of the world.

C. The third way of refuting an adversary according
to the Elenchos is to place him in the long chain of known

---

[17]Koschorke, Ketzerbekämpfung, p. 48, answers this
question with a clear no.

[18]I find questionable the way Koschorke,
Ketzerbekämpfung, pp. 22-55, regularly and without
qualification, equates 'regula' with 'system'.

heretics (<u>successio haereticorum</u>)[19]. Already present in the first two ways, this method is recurrent in the <u>Elenchos</u>, and is sometimes applied in an antonomous way. For instance, Callistus is thought to be refuted when Hippolytus has 'invented' heretical forefathers for him: Noëtus and ... Heraclitus (<u>Ref</u>.IX,7-12). Ultimately, these ancestors are always pagan philosophers, mystagogues, astrologists. Here again we find a systematic effort to deprive heresies of their Christian content. Such is the explicit objective of the <u>Elenchos</u> (<u>Ref</u>. I. prooem. 8-9) and all means are deemed good to show the un-Christian nature of heresy: artificial construction of genealogies, partial selection in the teachings of heretics, pure assertions, stereotyping, twisting of information, denigration, innuendos (most techniques studied by Koschorke).

The first heretics are assumed to be closer to the truth than those nearer or contemporary to Hippolytus. In this theory of the degradation of truth, Christian truth (or what Hippolytus holds for such) is identical with the truth of the primeval revelation. Some of this original truth was already lost in Judaism, but clearly more was wasted among the pagans--both barbarian and Greek. The heretics borrowed from the pagans and so lost even more of that truth[20]. And so, from one heresy to the other; the

---

[19]The method is already found in Jude's Epistle, according to F. Wisse, 'The Epistle of Jude in the History of Heresiology', in <u>Essays on the Nag Hammadi Texts in Honour of Alexander Böhlig</u> (ed. M.Krause), Leiden 1972, pp. 133-143. It also found an important place in Irenaeus, <u>Adv. haer</u>. I, and, without doubt, in Justin's <u>Syntagma</u> as far as his argumentation can be reconstructed.

[20]In <u>Ref</u>. I.prooem. 8-9 this view is clearly stated; it is said that Greek philosophers propounded more ancient and more august doctrines than those of the heretics (see also VII.36.2: 'It has been proved that those philosophers of Greece who have talked about the divine, have done it with much more reverence than these [heretics]'); but they also contained falsehood and errors to which the heresiarchs further added.

phenomenon is seen as a descending genealogy, in which truth kept being degraded and lost.

The three ways of refutation were already present in Irenaeus. But in Adv. haer. they had a subordinate role; they did not replace argumentation and refutation, which occupies four of the five Books of Adv. haer. Hippolytus develops those ways to their utmost; he systematically looks for pagan precursors to the heretics, for the borrowings these κλεψίλογοι would have made from the philosophers, for indications of their pagan origins and sources. The refutation stops with this denunciation which is typical of the polemics found in the Elenchos.

2. The Basic Disagreement with the Gnostics

These polemical techniques give the Elenchos its form and reveal a specific understanding, on the part of the author, of what is required to refute the heretics. We want now to raise the question which concerns us primarily in this study and which goes beyond what is explicit in Hippolytus's exposition. Can we find in these techniques, which permeate the Elenchos, an idea of what heresy, especially gnostic heresy, is? Has the author perceived and expressed what he takes to be central and most offensive in the gnostic 'hypothesis'? Has he stated what is wrong with the philosophers plagiarized by heretics, and if so does he counter his opponents with an interpretation of Christianity that really takes account of the gnostic heresy?

Writing in the first half of the third century, using Irenaeus's Adversus haereses, -- especially Adv. haer. I.1-21--and producing a work similar in scope, the author of the Elenchos cannot escape a comparison with Irenaeus. Does the Elenchos assign some important role to the instances which functioned as norms and authorities in Adv. haer.? We have already said that we do not find in the Elenchos the broad exegetical and theological discussion which we encountered in Adv. haer. We do not even find any

real information on how the heretics intended to base their
views on scripture. The author systematically denies them
any real connection with the Bible in his effort to
denounce them as being heathens.

Further, we might have expected the author of the
Elenchos, if he were also the author of the Apostolic
Tradition, not only to see the tradition of the apostles as
normative, but to make it so. But the Elenchos betrays no
such a view, and the thesis of the alien origin of heresy
makes it totally unnecessary. An important element of
Irenaeus's argumentation against the Gnostics is therefore
missing here[21]; there is no explicit attempt to establish
that the Gnostics do not possess the apostolic tradition or
have departed from it. The author of the Elenchos does not
know of such a criterion. His only comment about tradition
is that heretics represent a pagan tradition; when they
clothe it in a Christian garment, they turn Christianity
into an extravagant philosophical game[22].

As does Irenaeus, Hippolytus knows of a 'rule of
truth' (τὸν τῆς ἀληθείας κανόνα... Ref. X.5.2), which he
wants to 'demonstrate' in his last Book. However, the
demonstration is disappointing in its sketchiness (Ref.

---

[21]A possible, but indirect, expression of that view of
tradition might be found in Ref. VIII.18.2 where it is
said that the Quartodecimans, 'on all other points [beside
the date of Easter], agree with all that has been
transmitted to the church by the Apostles'. Elsewhere
(Ref. I.prooem.6) the author of the Elenchos seems to claim
some authority for himself on the basis of his being a
successor of the Apostles. K. Baus in Handbuch der
Kirchengeschichte, I (Hg. H. Jedin), Freiburg 1963, p.
283, states: 'Der Sicherung der apostolischen Überlieferung
in der Lehre dienen die dogmatisch-antihäretischen
Schriften Hippolyts'. Such a statement not only pays too
little attention to the problems of authorship, but
obviously reads into the Elenchos concerns that are not
encountered there.

[22]Harnack took Hippolytus (and Epiphanius, as we shall
see) at his word when he saw the gnostic interpretation as
an acute Hellenization of the Christian message. See his
Lehrbuch der Dogmengeschichte, I, Tübingen 1931, p. 250.

X.30-34), a condition which we may attribute to
Hippolytus's lack of interest in a positive vindication of
the faith. Moreover, the rule itself appears to have
played no significant role in the foregoing refutations.
The rule seems to be an abstract entity in the Elenchos; it
never has the character of the 'rule of faith' found in
Adv. haer.--i.e. concrete, universal, apostolic, a rule
which represented a real insight into the Christian faith
and was contrasted with the gnostic 'hypothesis'. 'Truth'
is said in the Elenchos to have been complete at the
beginning, and only to that extent is it used as a
criterion to measure the degree of non-value of recent
heresies.

Should we then conclude that the points of reference
that Irenaeus used to establish the truth of his faith
(scripture, tradition, rule of faith) are all absent from
the Elenchos?

Irenaeus knew how to find in all gnostic systems the
'blasphemia creatoris' and the implicit many-sided dualism.
These points, for him, formed the core of the gnostic
'hypothesis' and became the privileged target of his
attack. Some two generations later, Hippolytus does not
show the same sensitivity. We have seen that he complains
once about what could be the 'emanationist circle' of the
Basilidian system (Ref. VII.27.11); but he never develops
this potentially interesting element. On the specific
issue of the demiurge and the accompanying denigration of
the creator, Hippolytus has little to say. But at one
point (Ref. V.27. 5-6) he does not hide his indignation at
the role left to the God-Creator of the Old Testament in
the system of Justin the Gnostic; Elohim appears to be at
the center of the section on Justin and his degradation
upsets Hippolytus. This point, however, remains
undeveloped. He does not comment on the central place of
the demiurge in the section on the Peratae, and on its
implications. The blasphemia creatoris is absent from the
report on Marcion (Ref. VII. 29-30), a surprising
omission, since its mention would be expected there, and

because sometimes the affirmation of the identity of God
and the Creator seems important to Hippolytus. Does he not
say that the Montanists, 'in agreement with the church,
acknowledge the Father to be the God of the universe, and
Creator of all things; they also acknowledge what the
gospel testifies concerning Christ' (Ref. VIII.19.2; see
X.31.6)? But again this affirmation receives no
significant development.

Let us ask Hippolytus what upsets him most in the
gnostic teachings. Of course, he is impressed by the alien
character of heresy; he might have had something relevant
to say about its connection with astrology, about its
proximity to anthroposophy and theosophy (see Ref. V.6.6;
V.8.38), and something on its link with Orphic literature
(see Ref. V.20.4-5). But two statements in particular,
because of their content and place in the work, might help
answer our question.

The first statement we should examine is found in Book
X and probably contains the 'last word' of the Elenchos.
Starting from Hippolytus's final exposition of the orthodox
doctrine (Ref. X,30-34) and looking back at his long
presentation of the 'many-headed heresy' (Ref. V.11), we
find that Hippolytus was particularly struck by the
dispersal and fragmentation of the divine which he thought
he was encountering in all heretical doctrines. Whether
the philosophers from whom the heretics borrowed posited
one or many principles at the beginning of the universe (as
summarized in Ref. X.6-7), their 'plagiarizers', the
heresiarchs, tended to increase the multiplicity at the
beginning (e.g. fire itself, for Simon, is not simple:
Ref. X. 12) or the scattering in the Pleroma (see the
recapitulation, Ref. X. 9-19). In addition to this, some
heresiarchs concocted their own heresy by combining
together many existing heresies (e.g. Ref. X. 29.1:
'Others introduced something new, borrowing from all
heresies...') or philosophumena. The multiplication of
fancied beings in the heretical systems, and the ensuing
multiplication of doctrinal tenets, might be due to the

work of an underlying emanationist principle; but this is neither made explicit nor worked out in the Elenchos. The Elenchos stresses the point the author thinks most suited to counter the heretical atomization of the divine. Ref. X.32.1 contains this major, and possibly passionate, counter-statement; it says: God is one, he was alone, he created everything. This essential truth was ignored by the philosophies which the heresiarchs followed.

The second statement to be considered is similar in nature and is found in Book I (Ref. I.26.3; it reappears in a summary in Ref. IV.43.2). It concludes the exposition of the doctrines of the philosophers.

> All [these philosophers]..., being astonished at the magnitude of creation, thought it [=the magnitude] to be the Divine itself. They gave preference to this or to that portion of the universe, but failed to recognize the God of these and Demiurge.

This same view is echoed in Ref. X.32.5, where we read:

> I consider that, for the moment, I have sufficiently exposed the points ignored by the Greeks who glorified with subtle words the parts of creation while ignoring the Creator. Taking occasion from these, the heresiarchs disguised the views of the Greeks under similar expressions and framed ridiculous heresies.

It is clearly stated here that the 'Greek vice' upon which heretics built their systems is the divinization of cosmic elements and the failure to recognize the author of the cosmos.

Both statements, because of their place in the Elenchos, frame the entire work and mark out its main line. Surely, it can be said that they constitute but a slight indication of Hippolytus's central concern. To us they express Hippolytus's dismay at that which he found lacking in his gnostic counterpart. Irenaeus was particularly incensed by the dualistic outlook of the gnostic heresy;

but Hippolytus is most offended by its divinization of the
universe or of parts of it, and by the ensuing dispersal
and fragmentation of the divine. The doctrinal consequence
of this heretical view of God is the amalgamation of
disparate tenets (see Ref. V.20.1) encountered in
heretical systems and described at length in the Elenchos.
The heretical view concerning the divine is no small
mistake; it amounts to atheism. For, in following the
pagans, the heretics show that they 'are without God in
their thinking, in their character, and in their behavior'
(Ref. I. prooem. 8: ἀθέους... κατὰ γνώμην καὶ κατὰ τρόπον
καὶ κατὰ ἔργον).

Does this displacement in vision from Irenaeus to
Hippolytus bear witness to the changes in the gnostic
movement from the second to the third century, when it
was increasingly divided into a plurality of small groups?
Or does it reflect Hippolytus's increased knowledge of
gnostic sources (e.g. of the so-called Sethians),
especially of gnostic literature closer to pagan
philosophy? Perhaps it was due to some change in the
tactics used by gnostic teachers. Or perhaps the shift
bears witness to Hippolytus's distance from his gnostic
opponents who might already have virtually disappeared.
Irenaeus himself knew real Gnostics; he undertook his
refutation at a time when the Great Church was indeed
engaged in the process of overcoming the gnostic movement;
but to him Gnostics still represented a threat--and a
personal one. This is no longer the case two generations
later. The gnostic opponents of Hippolytus have ceased to
be a threat to orthodox doctrine; they might eventually
serve the author as a pretext to further his case and,
possibly, to disqualify an enemy well within the church:
Callistus and his group, if one accepts Koschorke's or
d'Alès's suggestion[23]. But the Gnostics themselves

---

[23]A. d'Alès, Théologie, p. 78 states: '... destiné à
confondre l'Église catholique comme secte callistienne,
[l'Elenchos] semble avoir été surtout, dans la pensée de

represent no concrete and immediate challenge. This would
explain the abstract way in which the author deals with
the Gnostics and his insistence on their alien
character, saying that they derive their doctrines from
pagan masters.

But we may also see, from the change in attitude
encountered in the Elenchos that there is an evolution in
the style of Christian polemics. In retrojecting present
controversies into heresies of the past, the heresiologist
does not pretend to attack those past heresies as being
themselves present. He expresses a new conception:
heresies are already ancient, but they have a cumulative
aspect. Heresies of the past have become 'classical' and
continue to represent a permanent possibility in
interpretation; and, if seen as elements in a succession,
they also constitute a tradition, the heretical tradition
which, as such, is alive in the particular heretics. Such
a view already implicit in Justin, will emerge with still
more clarity from Epiphanius's work. The connection
between the Elenchos and the Panarion might be only
indirect. But both share the view of a heretical tradition
which, from the middle of the third century, gave its shape
to Christian polemics.

---

l'auteur, une machine de guerre, savamment adaptée à ce but
secret.'

III. EPIPHANIUS'S PANARION

The fact that the Elenchos very soon circulated under
the name of Origen might explain why later polemists--
particularly Epiphanius (310/320-402)--were not inclined to
use it when fighting against heretics. While pseudo-
Tertullian (Libellus adversus haereses, before 250) and
Filastrius of Brescia (Diversarum hereseon liber, c.380-
390) show some knowledge of the Elenchos, Epiphanius
ignores it totally, if one is to follow Hilgenfeld.[1] In
order to find a real use of the Elenchos by later
polemists[2], we must wait until Theodoret of Cyrus
(Haereticarum fabularum compendium, c.453) who, however,
ignores Epiphanius[3]; for Theodoret was too liberal to join
Epiphanius in collusion against Origen. All the polemists
from the middle of the third century, though, share their
reference to Irenaeus. They also refer in general to
Hippolytus's Syntagma.

Lipsius has shown[4] how Epiphanius took his
documentation from previous heresiological sources

---

[1]A. Hilgenfeld, Die Ketzergeschichte des
Urchristentums, Leipzig 1888, p. 73.

[2]The many references to Ref. given by K. Holl in the
GCS edition of Epiphanius (see note 8 below), it should be
recalled, do not intend to indicate Epiphanius's sources,
but parallels. That Epiphanius parallels the Elenchos is
no indication that he is quoting it; he might as well be
following the same sources as the Elenchos. In that
qualified sense we say that there is no 'real' use of the
Elenchos by Epiphanius.

[3]On these relationships, see Hilgenfeld,
Ketzergeschichte, pp. 73-83, and our chart in the
Introduction above.

[4]R.A. Lipsius, Zur Quellengeschichte des Epiphanios,
Wien 1865, p. 37. Lipsius's work is a study of Pan.haer.
13 to 57.

(Hippolytus's Syntagma, Irenaeus, indirectly Justin[5]), sometimes transcribing them word for word and thus preserving, for instance, large sections of Irenaeus's original (Pan. haer. 31 and 34, etc.), of Hippolytus's Syntagma (e.g. Pan. haer. 57)[6], and so on. Epiphanius drew from heretical sources as well, and he sometimes expressly mentions his own reading, investigation or experience; we might not like the caustic tone of his narrative, but we have no reason to reject a priori the information he is providing; so we have him to thank for first-hand information on Samaritan and Jewish sects, on gnostic, Jewish-Christian, Montanist, Marcionite, Manichaean, Arian groups[7], and important sections of their own literatures.

The Panarion[8] represents an intensive piece of work if

---

[5]There is, however, no explicit reference in Panarion to Justin's Syntagma. See Hilgenfeld, Ketzergeschichte, p. 73.

[6]See further on this point P. Nautin, 'Saint Épiphane de Salamine' in DHGE XV, Paris 1963, cols. 617-66631, esp. 627.

[7]See Hilgenfeld, Ketzergeschichte, pp. 80-82.

[8]Panarion (Ἐπιφανίου ἐπισκόπου κατὰ αἱρέσεων [ὀγδοήκοντα] τὸ ἐπικληθὲν παναριον εἴτουν κιβώτιον) ed. K. Holl, GCS 25, 31 and 37, Leipzig 1915, 1922 and 1933. Also PG 41 and 42. It is referred to as Pan.epistola and Pan.prooem. for the first sections; Pan.haer. for the sections on heresies; Pan.christ. for the section on Christianity; Pan. de fide for the concluding exposition of the orthodox faith. Only very short passages have been translated into modern languages (e.g. by J. Horrmann in BKV[2], Rh. 1, Bd. 38, München 1919, which contains Pan.prooem., Pan.christ., the recapitulations, probably not written by Epiphanius himself, and Pan.de fide 13.2-18.6.   G.A. Koch, 'A Critical Investigation of Epiphanius' Knowledge of the Ebionites: A Translation and Critical Discussion of Panarion 30.   Dissertation, University of Pennsylvania, 1976).   Very little has been published on Epiphanius's heresiology; see P. Fraenkel, 'Histoire sainte et hérésie chez saint Épiphane de Salamine d'après le tome I du Panarion' (=Pan.haer. 1-20), RThPh 12, 1962, pp. 175-191, esp. 176. A comprehensive study of Epiphanius's heresiology is expected to be offered by Mme A. Pourkier, maître-assistant at the University of

we consider that it was written between 374 and 377[9] and
that it covers 1,361 pages in Holl's edition. But
Epiphanius had thought of the plan of the Panarion for some
time[10]: to describe and refute the eighty heresies facing
the one truth like the eighty concubines of the Song of
Songs 6:8-9, who surround and celebrate the unique bride,
but have no part with her. The image of the concubines,
while absent from the sections on heresies (one exception
is Pan.haer. 80.10 and 11), is developed in the
introductory and concluding sections of the Panarion
(Pan.prooem., Pan.de fide); here the multiplicity of these
ambiguous figures is contrasted with the one 'perfect dove'
who represents 'our holy mother the church, its holy
doctrine, the one holy faith in truth' (Pan.de fide, 2,8),
and is called innocent and simple (Pan.de fide 21,1
'guileless') as opposed to the intricate forms of heresy.

The image of the concubines recedes in the sections on
heresies, esp. in Pan.haer. 21 to 80, where it is replaced
by that of serpents and reptiles to qualify the various
heresies[11]. As a matter of fact, Epiphanius seems to know
as much about serpents as about heresies; each heresy is
likened to one species of serpent and these are called by
their 'scientific' names[12]. The image of the serpent as

Dijon. - The translations given here are mine. A new
edition and translation of Panarion is being prepared for
SC under the direction of P. Nautin.

[9]P. Nautin, 'S. Épiphane', col. 626, assigns the dates
374-376. Photius, Bibliotheca, cod. 122 (PG 103, col.
404), remarks that Epiphanius's work is more comprehensive
than all those written till then against heretics.

[10]Ancoratus 12-13 (ed. K. Holl, GCS 25), which already
enumerates the eighty heresies with which Pan.haer. is to
deal.

[11]For an (unconvincing) attempt to explain the
transition from one image to the other, see C. Riggi, 'Il
termine 'hairesis' nell' accezione di Epifanio di Salamina
(Panarion t. I; De Fide)', Salesianum 29, 1967, pp. 3-27,
esp. 16-17.

[12]As his technical source on serpents, Epiphanius
indicates a certain Nikandros of Colophon who wrote on

the symbol of a being in contact with the devil might have
been suggested to Epiphanius by Genesis   3, where the
serpent is related to the origin of gnosis[13] and is the
spokesman of the devil; or by Luke 10:19; or by the gnostic
sect of the Ophites (see Pan.haer. 37) who revered the
serpent and saw in the serpent-devil the origin of
knowledge; or by his heresiological sources. At any event,
Epiphanius saw the tide of serpent-heresies as originating
in Mesopotamia and, through Egypt, reaching Greece and the
whole Mediterranean world. Obviously the analogy of the
serpents has a discrediting character, while it provides
the various sections with a unifying theme.

It is with a view to this second image that Epiphanius
gave his work the title of Panarion. In the common
usage, a 'panarion' designated a box used by an apothecary,
which was filled with remedies against snake bite.

---

serpents and reptiles, while others wrote on the properties
of roots and herbs to cure their bites: Pan.prooem,
II.3.1-5.   He also refers to the works of the
'physiologists' (οἱ φυσιολόγοι) (Pan.haer. 64.72.6). He
consistently tries to relate the various forms of heresy to
a precise species of serpents (see. Pan.haer. 64,72,3).

R.M. Grant ('Eusebius and Gnostic Origins', Mélanges
Simon. Paganisme, judaïsme, christianisme, Paris 1978, pp.
195-205) has drawn attention not only to earlier authors
who attributed heresies to the devil, but also to the
rather rare comparison between heresies and snakes (pp.
196-197) made before the Panarion.

How Epiphanius took his information on serpents,
reptiles, and antidotes from some form of 'Fachliteratur',
is shown by J. Dummer, 'Ein naturwissenschaftliches
Handbuch als Quelle für Epiphanius von Constantia', Klio.
Beiträge zur alten Geschichte 55, 1973, pp. 289-299, here
p. 293. He suggests further that Epiphanius found his
information already collected in a single scientific work,
'ein zoologisch-pharmazeutisches Handbuch' (p. 296).   But
the author of such a hand-book is said not to be Nikandros
of Colophon, for Epiphanius says much more on serpents than
Nikandros's Θηριακά . The author of Epiphanius's immediate
source would then be unknown; he would have written a
compendium based on Nikandros and other physiologists.

13See C. Riggi, 'La figura di Epifanio nel IV secolo',
Studia Patristica VIII, TU 93, Berlin 1966, pp. 86-107,
here p. 104-105.

Epiphanius's Panarion is thought to contain the medications for all illnesses threatening the true faith. These 'medicinal aids' accompany each of the sections found in Pan.haer.21 to 80 and are summarized in Pan.de fide 1-25 which, returning to the first image, sketches the features of the venerable spouse of Christ in the form of a commentary on 'una est columba mea, perfecta mea'; in it again, unicity is contrasted with multiplicity, and polemical rejoinders season the exposition of the faith.

The Panarion opens with a first group of heresies (Pan.haer. 1-20): pre-Christian heresies, or proto-heresies, with which Christian heresies stand in continuity. In this group the first four (Barbarism, Scythism, Hellenism, Judaism, named in reference to Col 3:11, according to Pan.haer. 8.3.3) represent the primordial religious conditions of mankind[14] and designate some alien influences thought to have given birth to Christian heresies, especially gnostic heresies. They are only sometimes called heresies or, together with Samaritanism, mother-heresies (Pan.prooem. I.3.2; I.5.2.; see Pan.haer. 80.10.4)[15]; the rest of this section reviews Hellenic, Samaritan, and Jewish sects. The second group of heresies (Pan.haer. 21-56) is chiefly composed of gnostic sects, presented more or less chronologically and arranged in some kind of filiation. The last group (Pan.haer. 57-80) presents more recent heresies, some of which represent divisions among the orthodox Christians themselves. Two

---

[14]See E. Moutsoulas, 'Der Begriff 'Häresie' bei Epiphanius von Salamis', Studia Patristica VIII, TU 92, Berlin 1966, pp. 362-371.

[15]These designations, as will be seen below, raise difficult problems as to Epiphanius's specific concept of heresy. One point is clear, however: while the Elenchos deals with philosophical schools only to the extent that they form the background necessary to the understanding of Christian heresies which depend on them, the Panarion clearly starts with pre-Christian groups, called, and treated as, heresies. Epiphanius's concept of heresy encompasses pre-Christian philosophical schools as well as Christian groups.

are emphasized: Origen and the Arians.   These heretical groups, while spanning the course of history, geographically cover the whole oikoumene.   Their succession constitutes a negative history of salvation (Unheilsgeschichte), a counterpoint to the Heilsgeschichte; it is not without an eschatological overtone, suggested by the fact that the number of eighty heresies, long predicted, has now been completed, and we stand at the end of history.   In Pan.haer. 1-20 both histories are characterized by the symbols of Jerusalem and Babylon, but this designation is not expressly carried through.   Such a general view of history seems to have been the basic presupposition of Epiphanius and to have provided him with a general framework into which the information had to be pressed.

Each of the eighty heresies[16] (arrived at, sometimes, rather artificially by compressing many heresies or sub-dividing some), especially those found in Pan.haer. 21 to 80, is presented according to a recurrent scheme (illustrated in the Appendix below) which generally goes as follows.

---

[16]We will see later in what sense the first twenty heresies, above all the first four, are called heresies. To be sure, Epiphanius is fond of numbers, but his computations are not without confusion. Thus in Pan.haer. 80.10.4, wishing to be more precise, he says the Panarion is about seventy-five heresies, of which there are five mothers; he mentions, however, only four (Hellenism, Judaism, Samaritanism, Christianity) from which individual heresies developed, and it is curious to include Christianity at this point.   But we have to look at the preceding passage where Epiphanius, more correctly, lists Barbarism, Hellenism, Scythism, Judaism, Samaritanism.

On the problematic number of 80 heresies, see S. Le Nain de Tillemont, Mémoires pour servir à l'histoire ecclésiastique des six premiers siècles X, Paris 1705, p. 507:   'Le P.   Petau remarque qu'il (Épiphane) fait une faute dans cette supputation, en ce qu'il compte comme des espèces particulières de sectes les payens, les Samaritains, et les Juifs, qu'il met en même temps comme des genres qui en comprennent plusieurs; et sans cela il ne trouverait pas son nombre de 80 hérésies'.

1)   Introduction of the heresy by name. When it goes
back to a known heresiarch, the author asks who he was,
where he came from, where he was active, what he taught.

2)   Exposition of the heresy, its doctrine and
practices.

3)   First invectives: these tenets are lies,
fictions, distortions....

4)   Refutation: this heresy refutes itself or is
refuted by truth.   The refutation contains apostrophes
abusing the heretics and questions thought to be
embarrassing; the reasoning is by way of dilemmas,
expressions of indignation, ending with the statement:
"Whoever has a sane judgment will see that..." and the
corresponding article of the orthodox faith.

5)   Further invective and analogy with one species of
serpents injecting the venom of heresy.

6)   Transition to the next heresy with imploration
for divine help.

As is clear from this outline, the Panarion, unlike
the Elenchos, maintains a consistent distinction between
the exposition and the refutation, although the exposition
itself is already biased.   This is particularly true for
the gnostic heresies to which we give special attention in
the following pages.

1.   Epiphanius's Objective and Method

Why did Epiphanius bother to establish a catalogue of
eighty interrelated heresies originating far back in the
pre-Christian era, many of which had long disappeared from
the scene, as he himself confesses (Pan.haer.   39.1.1.;
see also 20.3.1 and 4)?   For as well as the author of
Elenchos Epiphanius knows that not all of these sects
represent an actual threat.   Both know that it would be
pointless to attack past heresies for their own sake.   Is
Epiphanius then merely paralleling the procedure of the
Elenchos?

Epiphanius presents and refutes heresies that no longer exist because, first of all, he sees a link between them and more recent heresies. He is therefore as interested as the author of the Elenchos in showing that there is a successio haereticorum; the cumulative process of heresies following upon each other gives each heresy a density it would not have if isolated. The connection between heresies might be at times loose, but it is firmly stated by Epiphanius: between pre-Christian and Christian heresies, between Hellenic and Christian heresies (Pan.haer.9.1.1), between Christian heresies themselves originating from the Samaritans and Simon. Throughout the sections from Simon to Bardesanes and beyond, Epiphanius stresses the genealogy of error: from Simon to Satornilus, from Nicholas to the Barborites and the Ophites, from the Valentinians and Archontics to Cerdon and Marcion; then (without showing how, but with a strong conviction) 'a certain Tatian arose as the successor of these men' (Pan.haer. 46.1.1). Epiphanius rarely complains that he could not find out where one heretic came from (e.g. Pan.haer. 58.1.1: Vales). Despite many cases of forced filiation (e.g. Pan.haer. 46.1.8; 55.1.1) we are confronted with a global genealogy of heresies, of which the cumulative character clearly emerges. Christian heresy started with Simon, grew with Satornilus (Pan.haer. 23.2.1) and those who came after, each heresy following upon the preceding 'inanities' (Pan.haer. 37.1.1; 38.2.3), thus building up not only a mere succession of heresies, but a real traditio haereticorum.

Such an interest in the history of heresy not only bears witness to the fact that 'Ketzerpolemik' has become 'Ketzergeschichte', as Hilgenfeld formulated the development from the second to the third century[17]. It also shows that the very idea of a tradition of heretics has become a polemical weapon.

---

[17]Hilgenfeld, Ketzergeschichte, p. 2 and passim.

The origin of this development can be seen in Irenaeus's source for the section of his work dealing with heretics from Simon to Tatian (Adv.haer. I.23-28, to which I.11-12 should be added[18]). The trend becomes manifest in the Elenchos where the interest in history sometimes obscures the polemics itself. Harnack even saw here the difference between the author of the Elenchos and the previous heresiologists.

> Bereits in dem Werke des Hippolyt überragt
> das geschichtliche Interesse an der ganzen
> Bewegung bei Weitem das polemische. Während
> Justin, Irenaeus und Tertullian bekämpfen
> und nur darstellen, um zu bekämpfen, liegt
> es Hippolyt, weit mehr am Herzen, eine
> sachlich beleuchtete, genetisch erklärte,
> vollständige Ketzerliste zu geben und
> während die Bestreitungen der früheren Väter
> vor Allem der Widerlegung irgendeiner der
> gnostischen Hauptrichtungen dienen, läuft
> Hippolyt's Werk in eine Bestreitung des
> Noëtus und Callistus aus![19]

For Harnack this difference, clearly apparent in the Elenchos, was a sign that Gnosticism in the first decades of the third century had ceased to be a disruptive factor for the church.

More than a century after the Elenchos, this 'historical' tendency was even more clearly evident in Epiphanius's work, with the difference already mentioned, that the Panarion gives more room to the refutation itself. The tradition of heresy now forms a counterpart to the history of salvation since the beginning of mankind. One function of this history of heretics in the Panarion, as in

---

[18]See F. Wisse, 'The Nag-Hammadi Library and the Heresiologists', VC 25, 1971, p. 213.

[19]A. Harnack, Zur Quellenkritik der Geschichte des Gnosticismus, Leipzig 1873, p. 82.

the Elenchos, has been to provide Epiphanius's personal
enemies (Origen, Cyril of Jerusalem, Rufinus, even Basil of
Cesaraea[20]) with a cohort of bad companions, thereby
discrediting them in the eyes of the orthodox. Moreover,
by interpreting the whole tradition of the eighty heresies
through the image of the eighty concubines with its
eschatological resonance, Epiphanius is stressing how alien
the heretical tradition is to the faith of the church and,
for that reason, how firmly it must be opposed. While the
emergence of the eighty heresies had to be expected if
scripture was to be fulfilled (now we have seen them all,
implies Epiphanius), the same scripture had already
condemned them all. To this condemnation the analogy with
serpents adds: all those heresies have been inspired by
the devil.

While such appears to have been Epiphanius's implicit
intention, he frequently states his goal in studying these
heresies throughout the Panarion.   He enumerates these
'abominations' both to overthrow heresy and to give his
readers a distaste for it, shaming those who do these
things (Pan.haer.26.14.5; see Pan.prooem. 1.2.3). It is
'in order to make intelligent people conceive hate
(ἀπέχθειαν) for the heretics and abominate their wicked
activity' (Pan.haer.25.3.3).   To those who might still
entertain doubts as to his intentions in describing at such
length reprehensible acts and ideas, he says: 'Although I
am truly ashamed to speak of their disgusting practices...
still I am not ashamed to say what they are not ashamed to
do, with the intention, by all means, of causing horror
(φρῖξιν) in those who hear of the obscenities they dare
to perform' (Pan.haer.26,4,; see 26,3,9; etc.).   Such is
the anticipated effect of the long catalogue of peculiar
thoughts and scandalous practices: to frighten away the
readers, to horrify them, to cause disgust for all that
departs from the catholic truth.   Epiphanius's efforts

---

[20]See P. Nautin, 'S. Épiphane', col. 627.

would have been in vain if they do not produce this
Abschreckung[21].

This objective determines Epiphanius's method. The
method is disparaging to the point that, compared to
Epiphanius, the author of the Elenchos might look like a
model of fair play. Epiphanius is a past master in
persiflage, invective, abusive language. Heretics are
regularly called foolish, insane, wretched (see Pan.haer.
24.1.6; 24.2.1; 28.1.1; 44.3.1; 46.2.2 et passim.) Their
opinions are silly, their talk babbling, their conduct
obscene. 'O foolish and vain fables! For nobody who has
one ounce of judgment, would dare invent such things about
man nor about god. Indeed even Homer appears to me to have
been more intelligent' (Pan.haer. 33.2.1-2; see 42.15.1-
2). Epiphanius has no equal in the history of heresiology
for the art of insulting. His descriptions of heretical
sects give much room to slander (e.g. Encratites are not so
out of virtue: Pan.haer. 47.1.6), insinuations (e.g.
Marcion had corrupted a young girl: Pan.haer. 42.1.4;
Encratites travel with disreputable women: Pan.haer.
47.3.1), calumny (e.g. of Origen: Pan.haer. 64.2.1 ff.,
who is called unbeliever [ἄπιστε] in the sense of un-
Christian: Pan.haer. 64.66.1 and 5). Epiphanius even
plays on ambiguities: he introduces Origen in a section
that immediately follows upon one devoted to an onanist

---

[21]That Epiphanius aims at Abschreckung (deterrence) was
assumed by Hilgenfeld, Ketzergeschichte, p. 2: 'Da nun die
bereits mehr oder weniger veralteten Häresien in den
Ketzerbestreitungen mindestens zur Abschreckung fortgeführt
wurden, musste die Ketzerpolemik mehr und mehr zu einer Art
Ketzergeschichte werden'. J. Dummer, 'Die Angaben über die
gnostische Literatur bei Epiphanius, Pan.haer. 26',
Koptologische Studien in der DDR, Halle 1965, pp. 191-219,
writing on Epiphanius's gnostic sources, remarks (p. 209):
'Wir erfahren zwar eine Reihe von Titeln, aber sehr wenig
über den Inhalt der Schriften. Was Epiphanius weitaus mehr
an Herzen liegt, ist die Schilderung der kultischen
Veranstaltungen und Veranschaulichung der Gedankengänge,
die diesen zu Grunde lagen - beides zum Zwecke der
Abschreckung'. Epiphanius's intention of causing horror is
obviously not limited to Pan.haer. 26.

group (Pan.haer. 63) and nothing is done to dissipate the
ambiguity. Beyond all the use he makes of Irenaeus, what
Epiphanius appreciates most in his work, is Irenaeus's use
of irony (e.g. Pan.haer. 32.6.7; 24.8.1). Where he
reports on gnostic use of scripture, he insists almost
exclusively on their immoral and erotic interpretations.
The lengthy descriptions of scandalous behavior (Epiphanius
claims that he does not delight in them: Pan.haer. 26.3.4-
6) are thought to constitute an uncovering of evil and thus
are believed to form a sure argument. For how could the
innocent readers fail to be disgusted by such scabrous
heretics?

To be sure, it may be difficult to remain serene about
Epiphanius's means and method. Indignant historians have
formulated harsh judgments on his person and style; his
unfairness has been punished by a lack of attentive study
of his heresiology. There is, however, a pertinent
portrait of Epiphanius drawn by P. Nautin, which is worth
quoting at this point for its well-balanced character.

> Nous ne nous rendrons pas juges de sa
> sainteté. Du moins était-il un ascète. Il
> en avait le physique impressionnant....Il en
> avait aussi la psychologie, avec ses
> qualités, la conviction ardente, la force
> d'âme, et avec ses défauts trop fréquents,
> qui s'accentuèrent avec l'âge, comme les
> jugements sommaires et définitifs, les
> partis pris, la facilité à s'aveugler sur
> soi et sur les autres, au point de mettre au
> compte de l'amour de la vérité ce qui était
> pour une grande part du ressentiment, et de
> se tromper entre un Théophile et un Jean
> Chrysostome[22].

---

[22]P. Nautin, 'S. Épiphane', cols. 625-626.

2. The Gnostic Heresies

Epiphanius describes and refutes gnostic heresies in
Pan.haer. 21 to 56. How does he conceive of them? It is
not possible to answer this question without first looking
at his general concept of heresy since 'heresy' finds in
the Panarion an application that goes beyond the gnostic
heresies.

After the middle of the second century, the concept of
'heresy' underwent a process of increasing complexity[23].
For Justin heresy was almost exclusively gnostic. Irenaeus
saw heresy as primarily gnostic, but he also counted the
Ebionites (i.e. Jewish-Christian deviants: Ebionites,
Cerynth, Tatian[24]) among the heretics.   Hippolytus's
Syntagma had, along with the Gnostics, the patripassiani,
and along with the Ebionites, two groups of Montanists[25].
The Elenchos added on the one hand groups like the Docetes,
the Callistians;   on the other hand the Elchasaites;
finally divisions within the church itself gave birth to
heresies, and we come 'zu einem gewissen Abschluss'[26].
A new development of heresy and an added complexity
starts with the emergence of Manichaeism and Arianism. As
a result, the concept of heresy in Epiphanius is rather
broad, if not diffuse, above all when one considers that he
also deals with pre-Christian groups which he calls
heresies as well.

As has been mentioned, it is precisely the inclusion
of pre-Christian 'errors' among the heresies that gives
rise to the problematic character of Epiphanius's concept

---

[23]Hilgenfeld, Ketzergeschichte, passim draws attention
to this process.

[24]See Hilgenfeld, Ketzergeschichte, p. 342; see p. 162.

[25]See Hilgenfeld, Ketzergeschichte. p. 163.

[26]Hilgenfeld, Ketzergeschichte, p. 453.

of heresy.   Following upon P. Fraenkel[27], E. Moutsoulas[28]
states the problem in the following way: Nobody has so far
explained exactly 'warum Barbarismus, Scythismus,
Hellenismus und Judaismus manchmal als solche [i.e.
Häresien] bezeichnet werden, manchmal als "historische
Perioden"...oder auch als "religiöse Zustände"'.   Then,
contrasting Epiphanius's concept of heresy with that of
Irenaeus and of the author of the Elenchos, he argues that
there are cases in Epiphanius where 'heresy' has no
negative meaning, but rather a 'neutral-objective' one.
This is the case for the first four religious stages of
mankind; when these are called 'heresies', it is not in the
sense of 'Irrlehre' of a particular group, but in the sense
of 'Entfremdung von der Wahrheit'[29] of Christianity without
connection with any group or school.

The hypothesis of a neutral sense of 'heresy' in
Epiphanius has been challenged by C. Riggi[30] for whom
'heresy' is always negative in the Panarion, even where it
only means 'Entfremdung von der Wahrheit'.[31] His argument
makes wide use of the images 'concubines' and 'serpents'
which, applied to the eighty heresies, always have a
negative meaning: the eighty concubines always remain

---

[27]P. Fraenkel, 'Histoire sainte'.

[28]E. Moutsoulas, 'Der Begriff "Häresie"', p. 362.

[29]E. Moutsoulas, 'Der Begriff "Häresie"', p. 368.

[30]C. Riggi, 'Il termine', pp. 3-29.   His thesis is
found on p. 5: 'L'accezione è in Epifanio sempre negativa,
sia come deviazione dalla condotta cristiana che come
deviazione dalla retta dottrina, sia come errore dottrinale
implicito (nello scisma) che come errore dogmatico
esplicito (nell' eresia comunemente intesa), sia come male
dilagante per il mondo in maniera confusa che come
organizzazione diabolica di gruppo'.

[31]C. Riggi, 'Il termine', p. 5, n. 5: "Or questa non
ci sembra più accezione neutra!".   On the contrary, Riggi
emphasizes that (according to Epiphanius) each heresy is a
monstrous and venemous product conceived through a contact
with the devil (pp. 6-7).

alien to the spouse, the eighty serpents are always
monstrous and linked with the devil. Even this point is
not without difficulty; with the exception of a general
reference to serpents in Pan.haer. 13.2.2 and 20.3.3, the
analogy of the serpents is only applied to heresies from
Simon on (Pan.haer. 21 on). It is not applied individually
to the first twenty heresies, much less to the first four.
Thus, while the analogy of the concubines might generally
apply to the eighty heresies, that of the serpents does not
and is reserved for the heresies 21 to 80. Therefore
Epiphanius seems to use the term 'heresy' in a double
sense.

For this reason we are more willing to follow Riggi
when he distinguishes, within the range of a generally
negative meaning of 'heresy' in the Panarion, between a
narrow and a broad sense[32]. Epiphanius himself hints at
such a distinction when he says (Pan.haer. 8.9.1; 9.1;
see 2,3) that the Samaritans (heirs of the four previous
religious stages) mark the point where his exposition
begins to deal with heresy proper, since they are at the
origin of all heresies based on scripture. If we consider
this statement, in spite of some remaining confusion, it is
possible to say: for Epiphanius, 'heresy' in the broad
sense means any fragmentation of the primeval unity; or
any departure, wherever it is encountered, from the
primeval truth and life. Thus it is understood that
primeval truth is revealed truth transmitted orally,
identical with the natural law which, in its turn, is
identical with 'Christianity before Christianity' and with
God's will (see Pan.de fide 6,8); primeval truth became
manifest with the advent of Christ. 'Heresy' in the strict
sense means any erroneous doctrine based on a wrong
interpretation of scripture with its accompanying moral
aberrations; this sense applies to gnostic heresies. The
first four religious conditions of mankind, however, are

---

[32]C. Riggi, 'Il termine', pp. 12 and 15.

called 'heresies' in the broad sense, so that Hellenism and
Judaism are counted as heresies only insofar as they have
been contaminated by the Babylonian virus and fragmentated.
The first four religious conditions are affected by a
generally negative character, always being contrasted with
'Christianity which existed since the beginning' Pan.de
fide 6,8), thus illustrating the permanent fight between
light and darkness[33]; while they coexisted with faith and
natural law, they never completely coincided with them[34]
and, by comparison, were always found lacking.

How then does the character of the gnostic heresies,
in the strict sense, emerge from Epiphanius's description?
He operates according to a fairly clear definition of
gnostic heresies.   First, they never represent simply a
false doctrine, but also include wrong conduct. Heterodoxy
is always connected with heteropraxis. Such a view was not
completely absent either from Irenaeus's work or from the
Elenchos.   But only in the Panarion is the practical side
of heresy systematically emphasized.   The exposition of
orthodox faith in Pan.de fide will have the same double
emphasis on faith and practice, the latter tending to
asceticism.   The conception of heterodoxy as including

---

[33]See E. Moutsoulas, 'Der Begriff "Häresie"', p. 370.

[34]In general, 'heresy' seems to be synonymous with
diversity itself, multiplicty, division: e.g. when it is
said that, at the stage of Scythism, there was 'no heresy,
no diversity of opinion' (οὐχ αἵρεσις, οὐ γνώμη ἑτέρα καὶ ἑτέρα:
Pan.haer. 2.3; see also 1.9; 3.9).   In Pan. de fide 9-12,
the emphasis is put on the multiplicity of sects and
practices in India, Egypt, Greece, etc., providing an
illustration of the view that outside the Christian Church
the original unity is fractured.   However, the state of
affairs is not always so straightforward.   E.g., after
dealing with the first twenty 'heresies', Epiphanius says
(Pan.christ. 4.7):   'I have talked up to now about eleven
heresies', meaning the divisions among Samaritans and Jews
only, and refusing in this case to call the first stages
and the Hellenic schools 'heresies'.
The study of Epiphanius's concept of heresy, as one
can see, is a frustrating one; Epiphanius's views were not
always consistent, and his conflicting statements are
difficult--if not sometimes impossible--to reconcile.

heteropraxis might have been prompted by Epiphanius's personal experience with gnostic behavior or by better information concerning gnostic rituals; it can also be a mere polemical device. However questionable his view was that heresies originate in moral failure[35], Epiphanius saw the essential connection between religious belief and moral conduct; to his mind a doctrine would hardly be false if it were not accompanied by a wrong practice.

Moreover, from the sections on the Gnostics, we can understand what Epiphanius sees as the content of gnostic heresy. Selecting arbitrarily among scriptural passages, Gnostics speculate about genealogies, divine and cosmic. They talk about heavens and archons, Hebdomad and Ogdoad, about which they imagine all sorts of myths to give free rein to their curiosity, to their love for disputes and vainglory (Pan.haer. 24.10.6; 35.2.1-2). Through their fraudulent myth-making (Pan.haer. 26.1.2) the Gnostics deceive people. They say that the world was made by angels (κοσμοποιοὶ ἀγγέλοι ; this feature seems to be peculiar to the Gnostics), not by the true God, so that the material world is seen as evil. In it the seeds of light (or of the Soul) have been scattered and must now be gathered again. On that basis some (the Encratites and those who resemble them) abstain from the world and its elements. Others practice immorality on the same basis; they think that licentious conduct, far from polluting the soul, contributes to its liberation; these people know well that advocating immorality is an appealing propaganda device (Pan.haer. 24.3.8; 25.2.1). Concerning Christ, they teach one form or the other of docetism. Finally they proclaim

---

[35]See C. Riggi, 'Il termine', p. 25. The connection established between heresy and libertinism is as old as Christian heresiology. See F. Wisse, 'The Epistle of Jude in the History of Heresiology', Essays on the Nag Hammadi Texts in Honour of Alexander Böhlig; ed. M. Krause, Leiden 1972, pp. 133-143, esp. 137 and 143; and 'The "Opponents" in the New Testament in Light of the Nag Hammadi Writings', Actes du Colloque international sur les textes de Nag Hammadi d'août 1978 (ed. B. Barc), Québec (forthcoming).

that there will be no resurrection of the dead (or of the
body).

   This picture of the Gnostics might be the product of
much fantasy on the part of Epiphanius and might result
from a systematic generalization.   It does show, however,
that he had a clear picture of them and it is against the
Gnostics thus understood that he thought he had to launch
his attack; for, like Irenaeus, he perceived the disruptive
character of those beliefs and was aware that Gnostics were
discrediting the church in the eyes of pagans incapable of
distinguishing between true and false Christians (Pan.haer.
27.3.3-5).

   To Epiphanius, gnostic heresies are rooted in grounds
alien to the catholic faith.   Building upon previous
heresiologists, he saw the gnostic views as having been
shaped by a series of bad influences: magic, astrology,
false reading of scripture, the devil's inspiration,
intellectual sickness, moral failure.   Among the immediate
bad influences, he gave an important role to Greek
philosophy and secular education.   Without being as one-
sided as the author of the Elenchos, Epiphanius saw the
false doctrines of the Gnostics as running parallel to the
false doctrines of the philosophers, with which they
entertain some connection.   For instance, for him the root
of the heresy of the Secundians (Pan.haer. 32.3.8) lies in
'their excessive education in the liberal arts and
sciences, and in Platonic thought' (δἰ ὑπερβολὴν δὲ τῆς ἐκείνου
παιδείας, ἐγκυκλίου τε καὶ Πλατωνικῆς).   The clearest
statements of this view will be found in the section on
Origen[36].   'You, Origen, you have been bit by a wicked

---

[36]Strangely enough, Origen is seen as the father of all
heresies and the instigator of Arianism (see Pan.haer.
64.4.2; 76.3.5; Epiphanius's letter to John of Jerusalem,
in Jerome, Epistola 51, PL 22, cols. 517-526, or PG 43,
cols. 379-390; see also D. Amand, Fatalisme et liberté dans
l'antiquité grecque, Louvain/Paris, 1945, p. 451).
Epiphanius's relation to Origenism has been studied by J.F.
Dechow, 'Dogma and Mysticism in Early Christianity.
Epiphanius of Cyprus and the Legacy of Origen'.

viper, I mean your wordly instruction...' (κοσμικῆς προ-
παιδείας   ) (Pan.haer. 64.72.5). 'You too, the Hellenic
education (Ἑλληνικῆς παιδείας) has made you blind for
the truth...' (Pan.haer. 64.72.9).

The thesis of the dependence of heresy upon Hellenic
philosophy was only pointed to marginally by Irenaeus
(Adv.haer. II. 14.1-6) who positively resorted to
philosophy throughout his Book II. After being generalized
by the author of the Elenchos, the thesis is now willingly
received by Epiphanius. The thesis is now applied not only
to the Gnostics, but beyond them, to Origen as well as to
the Arians. Without distinguishing between use and abuse,
Epiphanius is not far from counting philosophy among the
devil's inventions. Philosophic schools, as well as
gnostic sects, are called heresies (Pan.haer. 5-8) for
having introduced divisions among men. Not only is
philosophy thereby rejected, but also all links between
Christian thought and the ancient philosophical
tradition[37]. The ascetic Epiphanius can only see a sharp
opposition between 'Antike und Christentum'[38]; to attenuate

---

Dissertation, University of Pennsylvania, 1975. Origen
embodies most of the errors reviewed in Panarion.
Epiphanius had been so manipulated by Theophilus of
Alexandria that he conceived a most violent hostility
against Origen and devoted to him his longest notice (122
pages in Holl's edition, more than are reserved to the
Arians or to the Manichaeans). Accumulating massive
distortions upon formulations taken out of their contexts,
Pan.haer. 64 on Origen is but an amplification and
aggravation of the De resurrectione of Methodius of
Olympus, from which large sections are quoted (64.12-62).
On this see M. Villain, 'Rufin d'Aquilée. La querelle
autour d'Origène', RechSr. 27, 1937, pp. 5-37, esp. p. 8.
On Epiphanius's sources for the biography of Origen, see P.
Nautin, Origène I. Sa vie et son oeuvre, Paris 1977, pp.
202-217.

[37]Epiphanius's negative attitude toward images is
consistent with this view. See Jerome, Epistola 51.9.

[38]See W. Schneemelcher, 'Epiphanius von Salamis', RAC
V, Stuttgart 1960, pp. 909-927, esp. pp. 910, 923-926. F.
Wisse has proposed a further explanation for Epiphanius's
nervousness toward Hellenism. He suggests that

this opposition would amount to an illegitimate compromise.
Such an intransigent attitude is not limited to the
intellectual spheres of heretical doctrine; it also bears
on the concrete 'heretics' who, in the mind of such a
heresiologist, have no rights (Epiphanius is the one who
denounced a group of Gnostics in Egypt and had them driven
out of the city: Pan.haer. 26.17.9[39].

Does our discussion lead us to think that Epiphanius
had a clear insight into gnosis and gnostic doctrine? Did
he really understand gnosis? He surely perceived some
important tenets of the gnostic sects. But it is difficult
at this point to say whether he was able to perceive their
unifying principle, to relate the tenets to each other, and
especially to a fundamental gnostic insight. He sometimes
freely applies these tenets to different sects, just in
order to round out the picture and make it as repulsive as
possible. For instance, talking about the Nicholaitans,
but short of information on them, he explicitly borrows the
lacking information from other sects (Pan.haer. 25.2.1-5).
This kind of extrapolation often gives his reports the
character of abstractions, in spite of the heavy
accumulation of odd sayings and scandalous details.

At first glance, it seems that Epiphanius is not
looking for a real insight into gnosis, the way Irenaeus,
or even the author of the Elenchos, was. To him, indeed,
gnostic views are utterly irrational. He repeatedly

Epiphanius's attitude might very well reflect the horror of
the Christians in face of Emperor Julian's attempt at
making paganism, or Hellenism in the religious sense, into
the state religion (361-363). The revival of paganism that
had taken place some fifteen years before the writing of
the Panarion would have left vivid traces in the psyche of
church leaders. Gregory of Nazianzus exemplifies how a
Christian of a different character from Epiphanius's could
also remain haunted by the figure of Julian and his
demonic enterprise. See J. Bernardi, 'Un réquisitoire:
Les invectives contre Julien de Grégoire de Nazianze in
L'Empereur Julien. De l'histoire à la légende (eds. R.
Braun and J. Richer), Paris 1978, pp. 89-98.

[39]See S. Le Nain de Tillemont, Mémoires X, p. 488.

returns to this judgment. The devil 'always appeals to
feminine imaginations, pleasure and lust, that is to say,
to the feminine ignorance which is in men, and not to the
solid reason...' (Pan.haer. 37.2.5). Gnostics 'think the
things they are introducing are mysteries, although they
are nothing but mockeries of mimes (μιμολογήματα)
full of absurdity and nonsense. For these are truly myths'
(Pan.haer. 37.3.1-2). Such judgments obviously fall short
of indicating the precise points to which Epiphanius took
exception in the gnostic doctrines.

We can best discover what, for Epiphanius, constitutes
the unacceptable core of gnostic teachings by following an
indirect path. Instead of looking at his exposition of
gnostic systems, we may find the points that offended him
by examining his refutation.

3. The Core of the Refutation

In most sections dealing with gnostic heresies the
refutation, is introduced by two recurrent formulae.
'These opinions refute themselves', 'these opinions are
refuted by truth'. The first formula can be spelled out in
the following way: '... Madness refutes itself, and
wickedness is broken in itself internally, turning into its
own overthrow. But truth is always steadfast; it has no
need for aid, but is self-confirming, and is confirmed
constantly' (Pan.haer. 44.1.3; see also 21.6.1; 25.5.4;
26.3.2; 31.34.1; etc.). The second formula is encountered
in many variations of the following form: 'It is evident,
Bardesanes, how badly you have misplaced your confidence;
the truth itself is your refutation'. (Pan.haer. 56.2.11;
see also 21.5.1; 24.8.8;   24.9.1; 56.2.12; etc.). Each
time the formula not only introduces and qualifies the
refutation, but also amounts to a summary of it. Although
the contents of both formulae at times overlap, we should
consider them separately.

'Heresy refutes itself'

     What is meant by such a formula, is that there is no
need for any sophisticated argumentation in order to
overthrow the opinions just presented. 'There is, I dare
say, no use for any intelligent person to refute these
things from scripture, or from examples, or any other fact.
Their foolish fiction and adulterous action is obvious and
easily detected by right reason' (<u>Pan.haer.</u> 26.3.2). The
appeal to sound judgment is but a weak echo of Irenaeus's
argument by reason. In Epiphanius's mind it is superfluous
to develop a real argument in order to refute the heresy,
especially when the heresy has just been presented in an
inimical way that does part of the work of refutation. In
this instance Epiphanius deems it sufficient to point to
the quality of the opinions, of the author of these
opinions, and of the behavior connected with them. The
opinions are said to be inconsistent, contradictory,
laughable; they rest on a wrong or partial reading of
scripture. The author of these opinions is called an
impostor, a fraud, a deceiver, a fanatic, a sycophant, and
the like. The related behavior is corrupt, obscene,
filthy, insane.... Is it not right, then, to compare such
a doctrine to the spite of an evil serpent?

'Truth is your refutation'

     The content of the second formula is less
straightforward. In order to grasp the meaning of this
formula, it is useful to recall Epiphanius's fundamental
presupposition. His attack on heresies is based on a
vision of a universal history of truth and error[40]. The
whole tradition of truth--truth that has existed since the
beginning as the truth of the Christian Church[41]--is called

---

     [40]See P. Fraenkel, 'Histoire sainte', pp. 188-191.

     [41]Only rarely does Epiphanius mean rational or
philosophical truth. As example, we might quote the notice

upon to give the lie to the tradition of error. Thus,
after saying 'Truth is your refutation', Epiphanius
regularly refers to Moses, the prophets, the Savior, the
gospels, the apostles;   that is, to scripture (see
Pan.haer. 44.4.3).

The first meaning of the formula is therefore: the
truth of scripture is your refutation, thus echoing
Irenaeus's refutation by scripture. The spelling out of
such a refutation by Epiphanius will then follow a
consistent pattern: Heretics distort scripture, here is
the right text, here is a further text against their
interpretation. The procedure is best illustrated by the
long section of Marcion (Pan.haer. 42). Here Epiphanius
takes the trouble of quoting from Marcion's mutilated
scripture (78 passages from Luke, 40 passages from Paul).
Then after pointing to the changes made in these texts by
Marcion, or to variants when needed, Epiphanius
demonstrates, 'from the very remnants of scripture which
Marcion retains' (42.9.5), the truth for which the church
stands: incarnation, agreement of the two Testaments, God-
creator, inspiration of the prophets, divinity of Christ.
The texts retained by Marcion suffice to refute him; truth
itself refutes him. Of course, the rest of scripture which
is rejected by Marcion confirms Epiphanius's position.

When the disagreement with the Gnostics is rather a
matter of interpretation of scripture, Epiphanius tends to
side with the literal and "simple" interpretation of

---

on Stoicism (Pan.haer. 5) which has been studied by D.
Amand, Fatalisme, pp. 440-460. Amand shows how weak
Epiphanius is when he engages on philosophical matters.
His exposition is summary and inexact: Zeno of Elea is
confused with Zeno of Citium; Stoicism appears to be prior
to Platonism; the Stoics would believe in metempsychosis
(D. Petau has an indignant note on this misrepresentation
in PG 41, col. 201, n. 46). Epiphanius is following text-
books, and bad ones. His refutation is made of arguments
'd'une incroyable banalite' (p. 458), peppered with heavy
irony and cheap shots. His stronger arguments, such as the
moral arguments against fatalism, go back, as Amand has
shown, to Carneades and seem to have reached Epiphanius as
fossilized commonplaces (pp. 458-460).

scripture. For truth speaks in plain words (διὰ μικρῶν καὶ ἁπλῶν λόγων ἡ ἀλήθεια): Pan.haer. 35.3.2); for instance, scripture does not say that the angels are creators, or opposed to God, but it clearly says that they are his administrators and servants (Pan.haer. 40.4.2). To say more or otherwise is to imagine a fraudulent myth. Even the allegorical interpretation is included in Epiphanius's condemnation (see Pan.haer. 64.4.11). Those who do not stick by the plain sense of scripture are called impious (Origen is called ἄπιστε, as we saw), demons, prestidigitators, miserable.... They abandon the simplicity of the Holy Spirit (see Pan.haer. 69.71.1).

Thus when Epiphanius says that truth itself refutes heresies, he means a statement of the faith based on the literal sense of scripture. Moreover, this truth was found in the creeds which had been composed by Epiphanius's time. The council of Nicaea had produced such a creed, and Epiphanius was an ardent defender of Nicaea (see Pan.haer. 69.11.1). Furthermore, as Fraenkel mentioned[42], in the Ancoratus Epiphanius had already explained the faith on the basis of a creed that is one of the sources of the creed of Constantinople, 381 (see D 42-45). Moreover, when he attacks gnostic tenets or states the 'faith of truth' (πίστις ἀληθείας : Pan.haer. 24.10.7), Epiphanius reproduces the articles of the faith (the 'parts' of the faith: ἄλλων μερῶν τῆς πίστεως : Pan.de fide 21.1; τὸ πᾶν μέρος τῆς πίστεως: Pan.haer. 9.2.3), sometimes even in the order found in the creeds: trinity and unicity of God, creation of all beings, Christ's divinity and his birth from Mary, the church, the resurrection of the dead (see e.g. Pan.haer. 36.6.3-5; Pan.de fide 14-18).

It is the combination, then, of a literal reading of scripture with the articles of the creeds that will confound heresy. The venomous doctrine can be stopped with

---

42P. Fraenkel, 'Histoire sainte', p. 178. This had already been noticed by S. Le Nain de Tillemont, Mémoires X, p. 505 (on the two creeds concluding the Ancoratus).

the antidote of Christ's teachings (<u>Pan.haer</u>. 23.7.1-3) as
stated by the Church. This contrast hardly amounts to an
argument; it is, rather, an assertion briefly spelled out
and cast in a mold of invectives[43].

The preceding analysis should have made clear how the
style of refutation has changed since Irenaeus. Epiphanius
no longer carries on any serious debate with the Gnostics
by means of philosophical, scriptural, and theological
arguments. There is no longer any wrestling to determine
where the authentic tradition is. What we find, aside from
a virulent attack on all opponents, is a dogmatic appeal to
a static truth formulated in the articles of the creed. To
point out an inadequacy by means of the creed, it is
thought, is <u>ipso facto</u> to perform a refutation. We think
we have here the answer to the question we raised above:
what Epiphanius found most offensive in the gnostic
teachings was the low esteem in which they held the
explicit formulations of the faith. His interest in
doctrines different from his own hardly goes beyond
indicating them in a reproachful tone. His real interest
lies in reasserting the one truth as formulated by the
Church. Epiphanius does so with the firmness of one who
completely identifies himself with the Church that has made
such official pronouncements and with the Church that
receives these pronouncements with submissiveness. It is
from this double identification that Epiphanius seems to
derive the strong feeling of representing the majority.
From the same identification his style receives the
authoritarian, even at times arrogant character that
singles him out among Christian heresiologists.

---

[43]For an illustration of Epiphanius's style of
argumentation, see the Appendix to this Chapter.

Appendix: The Style of Argumentation in Pan.haer.27

We shall illustrate our comments on Epiphanius's style
of argumentation by presenting a paraphrase and summary of
the section on the Carpocratians (Pan.haer. 27.1.1-8.4).
It should be recalled that, for Epiphanius, heresies are
cumulative and build upon one another. Thus, coming after
Pan.haer. 25 and 26, which deal with many groups of
heretics (Nicholas and those connected with him) the heresy
of the Carpocratians is seen as a climax; it is presented
as having the most deceitful beliefs and immoral practices.
The refutation is cumulative, too, in the sense that it
refers to arguments already advanced against other sects
and still valid in the present case.

The section, reduced to its essential structure and
content, goes as follows:

1)   Introduction (27.1.1-2).   Then a certain
Carpocrates appeared.   He established an illegitimate
school in which to teach his pseudo-doctrine. His ways are
the worst of all. He contributed his share to the gnostic
heresy.

2)   Exposition of the doctrine and practices of the
Carpocratians (27.2.1-6.11).   Carpocrates splits the world
above into an unnameable Father and angels who created the
world.[1]   Jesus was born like all other men, i.e. from Mary
and Joseph, and was essentially like them, but his soul had
more power since it remembered what it had seen above.   In
order to show his power and to escape the angels who made
the world, he underwent all earthly experiences, including
lawless ones[2].   These experiences liberated his soul which

---

[1]Epiphanius takes creation by angels to mean that, for
the Gnostics, the world is evil (and the angels as well).
But this is not the Carpocratian interpretation, according
to which nothing is evil in itself as Epiphanius himself
reports below: Pan.haer. 27.5.8.

[2]Coming after Pan.haer. 26, this passage seems to mean
that Jesus taught the same licentious practices as those
attributed to the 'Gnostics-Borborites'.

reascended to the unknown Father.

Other souls will have the same destiny if they also go through all experiences. If they despise the practices of the Jews and perform even more sacrilegious actions than Jesus did, they might even rise above him through the strength of their souls thus manifested. To that end, magical and occult practices are welcome. Because these instruments of Satan call themselves Christians, they heap scandal upon the Church and discredit her in the eyes of the pagans. Furthermore, they spend their time in debauchery and perform all kinds of homosexual and heterosexual action with every member of the body, all kinds of filth and unnameable crime, thinking that if one performs all these actions during this life and leaves no deed undone, his soul will not have to be reincarnated; it will escape from the body-prison and be free. The body will not be saved. They dare to base such teachings on Jesus' words. Nothing is evil to them since no act is evil by nature. They use painted pictures and statues of philosophers, and claim to have portraits of Jesus made by Pontius Pilate. They worship them and perform heathen rites.

3)   Invective (27.7.1). We must resist these people by all means and refuse to pay attention to the teachings of such impostors. Some say: are not these teachings evidently foolish?   I agree.   But not only fools are seduced by foolish things; even wise men are led astray unless their minds are established in truth.

4)   Refutation (27.7.1-8.3).

4a)   They are refuted by themselves. (27.7.1-8) The arguments already opposed to Simon and his magical practices apply again here. Moreover, the doctrine of creation by angels is full of inconsistencies. Reasoning through a chain of dilemmas, Epiphanius affirms that such a doctrine makes the true God weaker than the angels. This is myth and fable. (The truth is that God himself created all things, visible and invisible.)

They say that the world and all it contains is
evil. But again they contradict themselves. For since a
part of the world, i.e. the soul, attains salvation, the
whole cannot be said to be utterly evil. If the soul can
be saved, it cannot be bad, though created by angels; nor
can the angels themselves be bad, from whom the soul
comes[3].

---

[3]As D. Petau remarked (PG 1, cols. 375-376, n. 92),
the refutation is not clearly in line with the exposition.
From the refutation it appears that Epiphanius attributes
two doctrines to the Carpocratians: 1. The world and all
created things have been made by angels, not by the good
supreme God. 2. The world and all that is contained in it
are counted among the evils. - Epiphanius refutes both
points. First, this would make God weaker than angels;
second, since a part of the whole universe attains
salvation, the whole cannot entirely be excluded from the
good. - But the second statement contradicts the exposition
according to which Carpocratians hold that nothing is evil
by nature. This shows that this refutation is thought to
apply to other groups as well. Epiphanius attacks elements
he has not clearly stated; similarly, he fails to attack
many elements he has presented. The inconvenience implied
in such a procedure loses some of its substance if we keep
in mind the cumulative character of both heresies and
refutations.
       However, this procedure obviously does not lend itself
to providing accurate and reliable information on the
groups Epiphanius is describing. Further, Epiphanius's
method of dealing with his sources gives rise to so many
inconsistencies that we are often confronted with the
impossibility of understanding what he is saying. Some of
the problems connected with Epiphanius's method are
analysed by R.M. Hübner, 'Die Hauptquelle des Epiphanius
(Pan.haer. 65) über Paulus von Samosata', ZKG 90, 1979, pp.
55-74. Hübner states, after comparing Epiphanius and his
main source for Pan.haer. 65, Pseudo-Athanasius: 'Diese
Gegenüberstellung [von Epiphanius und Ps-Athanasius] zeigen
immerhin, warum man den Epiphanius an vielen Stellen nicht
verstehen kann. Das dürfte auch für andere Kapitel des
Panarions ... lehrreich sein' (p. 69). The result of
Hübner's analysis, a contribution to 'eine umfassende
Quellenanalyse' (p. 58), is that Pan.haer. 65 is 'ohne
Quellenwert' (pp. 58, 71). 'Auf die Berichte des
Epiphanius [ist] kein Verlass, solange er uns seine Quelle
nicht nennt' (p. 72). Hübner even thinks he has caught
Epiphanius in the act of 'Fälschung' (p. 72) of documents,
thus concluding a severe analysis with a negative verdict.

4b) <u>They are refuted by truth</u> (27.8.1-3).
The same argument is illustrated by scripture and by the
case of Jesus.   Whoever has a solid mind must recognize
that there is nothing more foolish than Carpocrates'
factory of lies.   For if Jesus was born from Joseph and
Mary, as they say, and if he attained salvation, then not
only must Joseph and Mary themselves be saved, but the
demiurge also--that is the angel who made them--can no
longer be called deficient; for through them Jesus
proceeded from the Father.   If it is said that Jesus came
from the angels, this theory is reduced to the same
absurdity as was shown above.   (The truth is that Jesus was
born of the virgin Mary, etc.)

5)   <u>Invective and analogy with serpents</u> (27.8.3).
Such mythmaking (δραματυργὴμα) will not stand up.   It is
filled with spite and poisonous (ἰῶδους) doctrine.

6)   <u>Transition to the next heresy</u> (27.8.4).   We will
return to this heresy again later.   After throwing it down
like the head of a dragon with the help of the stick of
faith and truth, we turn to other monsters and hasten to
their destruction as promised (with the help of God).

CONCLUSION: CHRISTIAN POLEMICS AND
THE EMERGENCE OF ORTHODOXY

The idea that the polemical works of early Christian
writers resulted in the overthrow of heresies would
doubtless betray an inflated confidence in words -- and in
angry words. We can concede that Irenaeus had some
influence on relegating the Gnostics to the margin of the
Great Church; he even refused, probably in imitation of
Justin, to grant them the name of 'Christians'. But he
enjoyed such influence less by the force of the arguments
used to counter his opponents (arguments at times quite
sophisticated and difficult to appreciate fully) than by
the broad theology he developed in the course of his
attack. Furthermore, even before he started his work the
Church was already engaged in the victorious process that
was to lead to the triumph of a main stream. That is,
orthodoxy did not develop directly or exclusively from the
polemics against heresies. If we look at the period and
the situation in perspective, we can state that orthodoxy
developed out of a network of concrete decisions which the
Church made in situations of conflict such as the
confrontation with the Gnostics.

With this we subscribe to Harnack's judgment that
the gnostic movement erased itself from the book
of history[1]. Assuredly our judgment, as well as Harnack's,

---

[1]A. Harnack, _Zur Quellenkritik des Gnosticismus_,
Leipzig 1873, p. 81: 'Diese (= die gnostische Spekulation)
hat sich selbst, freilich einem zwingenden
Entwicklungsgesetze folgend, ausgestrichen aus dem Buche
der Geschichte'.
Tne same view was expressed by E. Schwartz in 1908:
'Diese (antignostische) Polemik ist es nicht gewesen, was
ihr (der Kirche) den Sieg brachte, sie setzt sogar, wenn
die spärliche und chronologisch unsichere Überlieferung
nicht täuscht, mit voller Kraft erst ein, nachdem der Kampf
entschieden ist' (quoted by K. Koschorke, _Hippolyts
Ketzerbekämpfung und die Polemik gegen die Gnostiker_,
Wiesbaden 1975, p. 93).

is to some extent conditioned by the presentation of the heresiologists. Gnostic literature in general, however, whether incorporated in patristic writings or encountered in the Nag Hammadi library, lends support to that judgment. Owing to its extravagance and esoteric character, the gnostic movement did not appeal to large segments of the population. It was incapable of--and perhaps uninterested in--representing a mainstream position. Seen in retrospect, a principle of fragmentation was too active within the gnostic movement for it to become a rallying center. Because Christianity was aware of the universality of its message from its earliest stages, and because Christianity perceived Gnosticism as an obstacle to its becoming a universal religion, the gnostic movement was forced to recede. But the movement did not wane without having allowed Christian polemics to find and develop their own style. It is with this point that the following observations are concerned.

1. The first observation that our analysis suggests concerns the evolution of the style of Christian polemics. In considering the sequence of three centuries of polemics, represented here by our three authors, one cannot help being struck by the decline of argumentation (of 'sachliche Auseinandersetzung'). Irenaeus had fixed the general pattern of exposition-refutation for his discussion of gnostic views. The exposition took the form of a compendium of views to be criticized and was already somewhat biased. The refutation, however, was developed for its own sake and had a broad basis anchored in rational and scriptural elements, the conjunction of which resulted in theological argumentation. In the Elenchos the refutation is included in the exposition which is thus made to serve a highly problematic thesis, that of the reducibility of gnostic views to pagan philosophy. A refutation does appear in the Panarion, but either as invective--the content of which is no more rational than the heretical doctrines just exposed by Epiphanius--or as a reminder of Church doctrine as formulated in offical

pronouncements to which the 'stubborn' heretics refused to conform. We can therefore say that the development of Christian polemics is marked by dialectical impoverishment. However disappointing such a result might be, it cannot fail to be instructive. It mirrors the changes in the situation that occurred from the time of Irenaeus and that increasingly made the heresiologist write an impressive attack against enemies who were more abstract and less threatening, rather than ponder over an argument and put it to use in an actual debate.

2. There is no doubt that the three works we have studied reflect the emergence of clichés in the battle against heretics. The caricaturing of one's opponents and their views is not, to be sure, an invention of the Christian polemists. But in their works it receives a role of increasing importance. The polemists maliciously cut statements from their context; they are not averse to focussing on questionable manifestations of heresy. We shall not enumerate all the cliches thus encountered; most of them can easily be gathered from the previous chapters. But we do wish to emphasize here the portrait of the heresiarch (and consequently of the heretics) as it appears at the end of three centuries of polemics.

It has been argued that, by the beginning of the second century, the tendency of Christian polemists was to identify the heresiarch with the traditional picture of the eschatological false prophet[2]. Starting with the end of the second century, this eschatological aspect progressively fades out. But a certain connection with the devil remains and the heresiarch keeps his character of false prophet and false teacher. This dark side will be developed to its ultimate possibilities. Increasingly, in the writings we have considered, the heresiarch is regarded

---

[2]F. Wisse, "The Epistle of Jude in the History of Heresiology" in Essays on the Nag Hammadi Texts in Honour of Alexander Böhlig, ed. M. Krause, Leiden 1972, pp. 133-143.

as demented, anxious to make himself conspicuous by his odd
ideas. He is filled with evil intentions (to break the
unity of the community, to make other people sick also, to
give free rein to their pride, etc.). In this way the
heresiarch does the devil's will; he is inspired, possessed
by the devil[3]. It is not surprising then that when he
speaks, he can only utter blasphemies.

This connection with the devil explains why the
heresiarch is not only a mentally sick person; through a
'procès d'intention' the heresiarch is declared a morally
debased being. The immorality of the heresiarch is
complete; it goes from advocating sexual licence, even
full-fledged libertinism, human sacrifice and ritual crime,
to the furthering of a 'morbid' rigorism and encratism.
Heresy is always the product of contamination of the soul
by the devil, and this contaminated soul expresses itself
in endless deviant ways. The features of the heresiarch
are shared in varying degrees by both innocent and vicious
followers alike; they have been injected with the same
contagious virus.

The portrait of the heretic thus becomes a caricature
of darkness and evil. He must be removed like an unhealthy
limb. Difference in opinions is taken to be a break of
unity, understood as uniformity; doctrinal uniformity was
increasingly perceived by leaders of the Church as a
strength amidst the vanishing Roman institutions.

The connection of heresy with moral failure (whether
heresy is born out of moral failure or merely accompanied
by it) and with mental weakness will henceforth be a
permanent feature of Christian polemics, though at times it
is only insinuated or suspected[4]. While this feature

---

[3] 'Organa satanae', as Justin already said, according
to Irenaeus, Adv. haer. V.26.2.

[4] Such clichés were not invented by the heresiologists.
They had already been alleged against the Christians by
their first opponents (accusing them of atheism, impiety,
debauchery, promiscuity, child-murder...). The
heresiologists only received those categories.

reflects the decline of argumentation in the works we have
studied, it will remain characteristic of Christian
polemics even when argumentation reappears in the 12th-13th
and in the 16th century.

     3. One significant characteristic of early Christian
polemics, with a considerable import for the following
centuries as well, appears clearly in the Elenchos. In it,
the very weapons that had been developed for use against
known heretics or pagans, are now bluntly turned against
brothers within the Church: in the Elenchos, against
Callistus; in the Panarion against Origen, among others.
The use of such a heavy arsenal against brothers who merely
differed with an author on unsettled matters seems to have
been an irresistible temptation for some authors,
particularly those who were weak in argumentation. Once
this arsenal had been used against 'gnostic brothers' who
initially thought of themselves as Christians, it could
easily be turned against any colleague who happened to
disagree.

     This phenomenon has its corollary: the transformation
of Ketzerpolemik into Ketzergeschichte[5] during the third
century. Heresiologists become less interested in properly
refuting individual heresies; these can be most easily
disqualified if by some way they can be assigned a place in
the traditio haereticorum. Then polemics as such tend to
recede and deterrent history becomes the polemical weapon
par excellence. This peculiar kind of history subordinates
everything to the goal of scaring people away from heresy
and of dissuading them from following heretics. The
polemist who writes this type of history freely uses
anachronisms to establish an impressive genealogy:

     P. Nautin has promised a study on the sources of
heresiology, which he thinks will be found in the
literature (primarily philosophical) of compendia and
epitomae.

     [5]As we saw above, these are the terms used by A.
Hilgenfeld, Ketzergeschichte des Urchristentums, Leipzig
1888.

attributions of recent opinions to ancient authors and,
vice versa, attributions of past positions to contemporary
authors.   That done, an essential part of the refutation
itself is viewed as complete.

4.   As a consequence of the change just mentioned the
concept of 'heresy' is broadened to an extreme degree.   We
can look at the polemical field represented in the three
works studied in this monograph as having a triple front--
against sectarian Christians, against Jewish sects, against
pagans (to which the Elenchos and the Panarion add a fourth
front against some fellow orthodox Christians).[6]   Irenaeus
distinguished these three fronts most clearly: first of
all the Gnostics are called heretics, then some Jewish-
Christian sects, but finally only Christian dissidents
deserve that name.   In the Elenchos, Jewish sects are
counted among heresies as well.   The concept 'heresy' is
then extended in the Panarion to pagans (although 'heresy'
has here a double sense as we indicated); that is to say,
the concept is used to embrace any departures whatsoever
from the position of the author and his fellows.   Such a
process made it necessary to postulate the event of God's
revelation always further back in history.   Likewise
Christ's revelation itself is pushed back (as in
Epiphanius) in order to make Adam the first Christian from
whom all heretics, past and present, stand in a position of
departure.

5.   A few remarks can be made here on the different
temperaments of the three polemists we have studied.   The
temperament of each author accounts in a certain measure
for the differences in their polemical styles.   Obviously
we cannot claim to be exhaustive on this topic, but wish

[6]We could visualize the situation as follows:

'Who is called heretic?'	Irenaeus	Elenchos	Epiphanius
pagans			X
Jewish sects		X	X
sectarian Christians	X	X	X

to emphasize the differences that appear to be most
telling.

We shall not repeat what we said about Irenaeus,
except that he tended to be, if not clearly 'conservative'
by temperament, at least decidedly moderate. He knew how
to oppose the extremes of moral and disciplinary rigorism,
as well as of doctrinal and speculative free-for-all. In
both extremes he suspected a subversive element that could
bring the Christian movement to ruin.

Because of the problems of attribution mentioned
above, the author of the Elenchos remains more elusive, for
we have to rely exclusively on internal evidence to reach
his character. But clearly he has a grudge against a lax
pope and against moral compromise. He hardly hides his
ecclesiastical ambitions and does not hesitate to show off
his learning and virtue in order to legitimize his
authority.

Similarly, Epiphanius has strong feelings against
Origen and the Origenists. In the Panarion he appears to
have an extreme dislike for doctrinal compromise. The
bishop of Salamis was very respected in his life-time; when
he writes against all those who disagree with the official
Church, he cannot hide a patriarchal view of himself. He
strongly feels that he has the majority in the Church on
his side and shows that he would not tolerate any
challenge. He seems to be more interested in crushing his
opponents than in persuading them.

To continue this reflection would lead to the futile
exercise of analyzing the psyche of our polemists. It
might be fruitful to see how such temperaments came to play
a role in the area of ecclesiastical politics that is
called the emergence of orthodoxy. However, we want to
consider the emergence of normative Christianity from a
different perspective.

6. We wish to conclude our study with some remarks on
the dialectics of emerging orthodoxy. These remarks will
use the content of the preceding chapters as a point of
departure.

We said above that orthodoxy developed out of situations of conflict in which the Church was called upon to make concrete decisions that would shape Christianity. If we try to say more about these decisions[7] and combine the perceptions of the historian with those of the participant, we can mention the following themes running through the first four centuries. Christianity did face these conflicts; seen in retrospect, the crucial and underlying issues can be formulated as follows:

A. Some of the situations of conflict, with an accompanying challenge for Christianity, were
   . encounter with Judaism: danger of remaining a sect; danger of losing its Christological distinctiveness;
   . encounter with the Gentiles: danger of losing its monotheistic distinctiveness;
   . encounter with gnostic groups: danger of losing its identity as historical religion; danger of becoming elitist and esoteric;
   . encounter with Graeco-Roman cults: danger of idolatry and syncretism;
   . encounter with the Roman Empire: danger of playing down its distinctive religious character; danger of overadaptation;
   . encounter with Hellenistic philosophy: danger of being dissolved into philosophic doctrines; danger of losing its historical character;
   . encounter with Roman law: danger of losing its prophetic and eschatological character; danger of structural assimilation.

B. Some of the concrete decisions that had to be made pertained to
   . membership: limitation or universality;
   . discipline: rigorism or 'indulgence';

---

[7]The decisions we have in mind here are those that the Church was forced to take before being able to account for them in a fully rational way.

- authority: scripture-tradition or Spirit;
                  hierarchy, college or people;
- doctrine: positivism or free speculation;
                  esoteric or exoteric;
                  elitist or popular;
- adaptation: partial or total;
                  rejection of Zeitgeist or coming to
                  terms with it.

The option for universality, present in the original
message of Christianity, determined the mission to the
Gentiles and provided an impetus for the admission of all
(women, slaves, civil officers, nationals, illiterate
people, philosophers, etc.). Such a movement might have
been favoured by the denationalizing of the Empire in the
2nd and 3rd centuries.[8] But Christianity truly became a
mass-movement when the Church decided, around the middle of
the 3rd century, to re-admit the lapsi[9]. It triumphed in
the second half of the 3rd century, before becoming the
state-church in the 4th century. If the drive toward
universality was to succeed, a 'centrist' mood had to
prevail. How could it have been otherwise? Extremist
groups which jeopardized this drive had to retreat:
reactionary groups (e.g. Judeo-Christians and, to some
extent, the Montanists), rigorist groups (e.g. the
Encratites, those opposing the readmission of the lapsi),
enthusiastic radicals or optimistic enthusiasts (e.g. the
Montanists), extravagant speculators or 'pessimistic
enthusiasts' (e.g. the Gnostics)[10] -- in a word, all groups

---

[8] See F.W. Kantzenbach, Christentum in der
Gesellschaft, Bd. 1, Alte Kirche und Mittelalter, Hamburg
1975, p. 90.

[9] See Kantzenbach, Christentum, pp. 74, 85-87.

[10] The Gnostics are characterized in this way by F.
Wisse,' "The Opponents" in the New Testament in the Light of
the Nag Hammadi Writings', in Actes du Colloque
international sur les textes de Nag Hammadi d'août 1978,
ed. B. Barc, Québec (forthcoming).

opting for some form of elitism.[11]   But even elitist
concerns will be slowly re-admitted under the Church's
umbrella (e.g. in monasticism) so that practically no
barrier will be put to universality once effective control
is established. Progressively, as can be seen in the 4th
century, that control becomes reducible to a control of
language.[12]

It was not only the drive toward universality that led
to the building of a wide centrist position. This broad
base is always necessitated by the development of any
society toward some form of institutional stability, upon
which the continued existence of that society depends. To
those concerned with both universality and stability,
pluralism is intolerable. The formation of a wide basis of
agreement is a necessity.

The development of a centrist position can be
considered from a different perspective. In the life of a
social group, three moments of crisis can be distinguished:
the crisis of existence, the crisis of relevance, the
crisis of identity.[13] Thinking of early Christianity, we
could, rather arbitrarily, assign dates to each of these

---

[11]See Kantzenbach, Christentum, p. 52.

[12]It would be instructive to compare the emergence of
orthodoxy to the contemporary formation of unanimous
communities and artifical societies, such as the communist
party, the societies of psychoanalysis, etc. This idea is
suggested to us by V. Descombes, Le même et l'autre.
Quarante ans de philosophie française, Paris 1979, pp. 124-
130. In such societies the function of a common language
is decisive to the point that the ascendency of the
institution over the individuals can be reduced to the
domination of a language. The social bond is so grounded
in language that altering the language is perceived as a
subversion of the community.

[13]These moments are suggested by J. Moltmann's
analysis of the contemporary scene in terms of relevance
and identity in The Crucified God, London 1974, pp. 7-21,
and by Th. Baumeister's application of Moltmann's analysis
to early Christianity in 'Montanismus und Gnostizismus',
TrTZ 87, 1978, pp. 44-60. Baumeister thinks (pp. 44-45)
that our time of rapid social change presents many
similarities with the beginnings of Christianity.

moments: the year 70 (the loss of the home-base), the year
135 (adaptation to the Zeitgeist and ecumenical momentum at
the time of Hadrian), from the year 150 on (need for
strengthening cohesion brought about by an adaptation that
might go too far, accompanied by the temptation to form a
ghetto against the dangers of dispersion in the surrounding
world).   Instead of thinking of these moments in an
historical sequence, however, it seems more accurate to see
them as complementary and permanent features of the
Christian movement in the first centuries. That is, the
existence of the Christian movement is always threatened by
persecutions; the need for adaptation is present as soon as
the movement turns to the Gentiles and becomes aware of its
universal character; the awareness of being different (as
well as being most 'ancient') is expressed in the original
message and will be constantly affirmed.

While the drive toward orthodoxy is realized through
moments determined by both the crisis of relevance and that
of identity, it seems to stand closer to the latter. Once
the Christian movement succeeded in maintaining itself and
in establishing a large social basis in the Roman world,
once it reached a degree of self-confidence and certainty
about its future, the need to affirm this distinctiveness
was felt in a renewed way. Excessive concern for relevance
had to be tempered by an insistence on what constitutes the
specific difference and the unique character of movement.
In other words, the drive toward relevance and universality
is limited by the drive toward identity.

In the second and third centuries, the Christian
movement asserted its difference through a series of
exclusions, rejecting elements felt to be too extreme.
Total assimilation to the world and retreat into the
ghetto were both seen as threats to the very existence of
the movement. A number of possibilities on both extremes
had to be ruled out; again, but this time for the sake of
the movement's distinctiveness, a centrist position had to
be developed.

In order not to yield to a spatial view of the
emergence of orthodoxy, we may express the same idea more
accurately in other words. Identity is constituted through
a series of partitions whereby it is affirmed that
'reality' has to be separated from 'dream', 'truth' from
'arbitrariness', 'old' from 'new', 'reason' from 'folly'--
in short, 'we' from 'others'. In order for a group to make
those partitions, it must have reached a stage of
development which allows the talk about majority and
consent to have meaning and to correspond to truth-claims.
This is not the case in early stages of a movement, nor are
these stages the times in which concerns for orthodoxy
prevail. Such concerns do prevail when the group, which
might have had charismatic features in its beginnings, has
impressed its relevance upon masses and is in the process
of slowly becoming an institution. The strength of the
institution depends on the strength of its social basis;
its authority is expressed and enhanced by appeals to its
'antiquity' as well as to the 'majority' it represents; its
truth is founded on doctrinal agreements. But the
institution is also hypersensitive. It interprets all
disagreement as opposition. Since its truth resides in
consent, dissent forms obstruction to truth. If the truth
is to recover its integrity, the deviant has to recant, or
to disappear.

Naturally the criterion of doctrinal agreement and
consent is the ground of intolerance. Dissenters, because
of the vital threat they represent to the integrity, even
to the very existence of truth, have to be depicted in the
blackest terms. They are in league with the arch-enemy who
wants the ruin of the movement; they sell out the
distinctive character of Christianity to the pagans and the
surrounding world; they exclude the majority by being too
subtle, and so on. Because of the seriousness of the
threat they represent, dissenters have lost their rights to
exist in the Church, even to exist at all.

Orthodoxy was thus born in the wake of Christianity's
search for its difference and identity. Heavy sacrifices

had to be accepted as well as unfortunate losses. They did
not easily cease even after the search had succeeded in
achieving normative self-definition. In this light, it is
but a slight consolation to assert that

> it is indeed a curious quirk of history that
> western Rome was destined to begin to exert
> the determinative influence upon a religion
> which had its cradle in the Orient, so as to
> give it that form in which it was to achieve
> worldwide recognition. But as an other-
> wordly religion that despises this world and
> inflexibly orders life in accord with a
> superhuman standard that has descended from
> heaven, or as a complicated mystery cult for
> religious and intellectual connoisseurs, or
> as a tide of fanatical enthusiasm that
> swells today and ebbs tomorrow, Christianity
> never could have achieved such
> recognition.[14]

The more rigid orthodoxy appears, the more it loses
confidence that the movement is sufficiently powerful to
maintain itself,[15] until renewed search for relevance calls
it to a new opening to the world. The concern for
orthodoxy thus appears as a dialectical moment (the moment
of care for distinctiveness and identity) in the
development of a social movement; sooner or later it is
accompanied by another moment, that of care for relevance.
In this process the temptation consists in thinking that
orthodoxy, in one historical situation, has achieved the
perfect and final form of realization to which all
subsequent forms have to be measured and reduced. Needless
to say, such a temptation has never failed to exercise its
lure.

---

[14]W. Bauer, _Orthodoxy and Heresy in Earliest
Christianity_, Philadelphia 1971, p. 240.

[15]See Moltmann, _Crucified God_, p. 19.

BIBLIOGRAPHY

Aland, B., ed. Gnosis. Festschrift für Hans Jonas,
Göttingen 1978.

Aland, K. Kirchengeschichtliche Entwürfe, Gütersloh 1960.

d'Alès, A. La théologie de saint Hippolyte, Paris 1906.

Amand, D. Fatalisme et liberté dans l'antiquité grecque,
Louvain/Paris 1945.

Andresen, C. Die Kirchen der alten Christenheit, Stuttgart
1971.

——. Logos und Nomos. Die Polemik des Kelsos wider das
Christentum, Berlin 1955.

Audet, T.A. 'Orientations théologiques chez saint Irénée',
Traditio 1, 1943, pp. 15-54.

Barnes, T.D. 'The Chronology of Montanism', JTS 21, 1970,
pp. 403-408.

Baumeister, Th. 'Montanismus und Gnostizismus', TrTZ 87,
1978, pp. 44-60.

Bauer, W. Orthodoxy and Heresy in Earliest Christianity, ET
eds. R. Kraft and G. Krodel, London/Philadelphia
1972/1971.

Benoit, A. Saint Irénée. Introduction à l'étude de sa
théologie, Paris 1960.

Bernardi, J. 'Un réquisitoire: Les Invectives contre
     Julien de Grégoire de Nazianze', L'Empereur Julien.
     De l'histoire à la légende, eds. R. Braun and J.
     Richer, Paris 1978, pp. 89-98.

Blanchetière, F. 'Le montanisme originel I', RevSR 52,
     1978, pp. 118-134.

——. 'Le montanisme originel II', RevSR 53, 1979, pp. 1-22.

Bousset, W. Jüdisch-christlicher Schulbetrieb in Alexandria
     und Rom, Göttingen 1915.

Brox, N. 'Antignostische Polemik bei Christen und Heiden',
     MTZ 18, 1967, pp. 265-291.

——. Γνωστικοί als häresiologischer Terminus', ZNW 57, 1966,
     pp. 105-114.

——.   'Der einfache Glaube und die Theologie.   Zur
     altkirchlichen Geschichte eines Dauerproblems',
     Kairos 14, 1972, pp. 161-187.

——. 'Juden und Heiden bei Irenäus', MTZ 16, 1965, pp. 89-
     106.

——.   'Kelsos und Hippolytos.   Zur frühchristlichen
     Geschichtspolemik', VC 20, 1966, pp. 150-158.

——. Offenbarung, Gnosis und gnostischer Mythos bei Irenäus
     von Lyon, Salzburg/München 1966.

——.   'Offenbarung -- gnostisch und christlich'. Stimmen
     der Zeit 182, 1968, pp. 105-117.

Butterworth, R. Hippolytus of Rome: Contra Noetum,
     Heythrop Monographs 2, London 1977.

Bibliography

Carpenter, H.J. 'Popular Christianity and the Theologians
in the Early Centuries', JTS 14, 1963, pp. 294-310.

Daniélou, J. Origène, Paris 1948.

Dechow, J.F. 'Dogma and Mysticism in Early Christianity.
Epiphanius of Cyprus and the Legacy of Origen',
Dissertation, University of Pennsylvania, 1975.

Descombes, V. Le même et l'autre. Quarante ans de
philosophie française, Paris 1979.

Dillon, J. The Middle Platonists. A Study of Platonism 80
B.C. to A.D. 220, London 1977.

Doutreleau, L. 'Irénée de Lyon', DS VII, Paris 1971, cols.
1923-38.

Duchesne-Guillemin, J. 'Dualismus', RAC 4, Stuttgart 1959,
cols. 334-350.

Dummer, J. 'Die Angaben über die gnostische Literatur bei
Epiphanius, Pan.haer. 26', Koptologische Studien in
der DDR, Halle 1965, pp. 191-219.

——. 'Ein naturwissenschaftliches Handbuch als Quelle für
Epiphanius von Constantia', Klio. Beiträge zur alten
Geschichte 55, 1973, pp. 289-299.

Ficker, G. Studien zur Hippolytfrage, Leipzig 1893.

Fischer, J.A. 'Die antimontanistischen Synoden des 2./3.
Jahrhunderts', AHC 6, 1974, pp. 241-273.

Fraenkel, P. 'Histoire sainte et hérésie chez saint
Épiphane de Salamine d'après le tome I du Panarion',
RThPh 12, 1962, pp. 175-191.

Frend, W.H.C. 'The Gnostic-Manichaean Tradition in Roman
    North Africa', JEH 4, 1953, pp. 13-26.

——. 'The Gnostic Sects and the Roman Empire', JEH 5, 1954,
    pp. 25-37.

——. 'Heresy and Schism as Social and National Movements',
    Studies in Church History, ed. D. Baker, vol. 9,
    1972, pp. 37-56.

Froehlich, K. 'Montanism and Gnosis', The Heritage of the
    Early Church. Essays in Honor of the Very Reverend
    G.V. Florovsky, eds. D. Neiman and M. Schatkin,
    Roma 1973, pp. 91-111.

Gibson, E. 'Montanism and its Monuments', Dissertation,
    Harvard University, 1974.

Grant, R.M. 'Irenaeus and Hellenistic Culture', HTR 42,
    1949, pp. 41-51.

——. 'Eusebius and Gnostic Origins', Mélanges Simon.
    Paganisme, judaïsme, christianisme, Paris 1978, pp.
    195-205.

Green, H.A. 'Gnosis and Gnosticism. A Study in
    Methodology', Numen 24, 1977, pp. 95-134.

Greenslade, S.L. 'Heresy and Schism in the Later Roman
    Empire', Studies in Church History, ed. D. Baker,
    vol. 9, 1972, pp. 1-20.

Hägglund, B. 'Die Bedeutung der "regula fidei" als
    Grundlage theologischer Aussagen', StTh 12, 1958,
    pp. 1-44.

Harnack, A. Lehrbuch der Dogmengeschichte I, Tübingen
    1931.

——. Zur Quellenkritik des Gnosticismus, Leipzig 1873.

Hasenhüttl, G. and Nolte, J. Formen kirchlicher Ketzer-
    bewältigung, Düsseldorf 1976.

Hefner, P. 'Theological Methodology and St. Irenaeus', JR
    44, 1964, pp. 294-309.

Hilgenfeld, A. Ketzergeschichte des Urchristentumus,
    Leipzig 1888.

Hübner, R.M. 'Die Hauptquelle des Epiphanius (Pan.haer.
    65) über Paulus von Samosata', ZKG 90, 1979, pp. 55-
    74.

Jedin, H., ed. Handbuch der Kirchengeschichte I, Freiburg
    1963.

Jonas, H. 'A Retrospective View', Proceedings of the
    International Colloquium on Gnosticism, Stockholm
    August 20-25, 1973, Stockholm 1977, pp. 1-15.

Jones, A.H.M. 'Were Ancient Heresies National or Social
    Movements in Disguise?', JTS 10, 1959, pp. 280-298.

Kantzenbach, F.W. Christentum in der Gesellschaft, Bd. 1,
    Alte Kirche und Mittelalter, Hamburg 1975.

Koch, G.A. 'A Critical Investigation of Epiphanius'
    Knowledge of the Ebionites: A Translation and
    Critical Discussion of Panarion 30'. Dissertation,
    University of Pennsylvania, 1976.

Korschorke, K. Hippolyts Ketzerbekämpfung und Polemik gegen
    die Gnostiker: Eine Tendenzkritische Untersuchung
    seiner 'Refutatio omnium haeresium', Wiesbaden
    1975.

——. Die Polemik der Gnostiker gegen das kirchliche
Christentum, Leiden, 1978.

Kraft, H. 'Die lyoner Märtyrer und der Montanismus', Les
martyrs de Lyon (177), Colloques internationaux du
CNRS (20-23 September 1977), Paris 1978, pp. 233-
247.

Lebreton, J. 'Le désaccord de la foi populaire et de la
théologie savante dans l'Eglise chrétienne du IIIe
siècle', RHE 19, 1923, pp. 481-506 and RHE 20, 1924,
pp. 5-37.

——. 'Le désaccord entre la foi populaire et la théologie
savante', Histoire de l'Eglise 2, eds. A. Fliche
and U. Martin, Paris 1948, pp. 361-374.

Le Boulluec, A. 'Y a-t-il des traces de la polémique
antignostique d'Irénée dans le Peri Archon
d'Origène?', Gnosis and Gnosticism, ed. M. Krause,
Leiden 1977, pp. 138-147.

Le Goff, ed. Hérésies et sociétés dans l'Europe préindustrielle 11e-18e siècle, Paris/La Haye 1968.

Le Nain de Tillemont, S. Mémoires pour servir à l'histoire
ecclésiastique des six premiers siècles. X, Paris
1705.

Lipsius, R.A. Die Quellen der ältesten Ketzergeschichte neu
untersucht, Leipzig 1875.

——. Zur Quellenkritik des Epiphanius, Wien 1865.

Loi, V. 'L'identità letteraria di Ippolito di Roma',
Ricerche su Ippolito (collab.), Studia Ephemeridis
Augustianianum 13, Roma 1977, pp. 67-88.

——. 'La problematica storica-letteraria su Ippolito di
      Roma', Ricerche su Ippolito, pp. 9-16.

Markus, R.A. 'Christianity and Dissent in Roman North
      Africa: Changing Perspectives in Recent Work',
      Studies in Church History, ed. D. Baker, Vol. 9,
      1972, pp. 21-36.

——. 'Pleroma and Fulfilment. The Significance of History
      in St. Irenaeus' Opposition to Gnosticism', VC 8,
      1954, pp. 193-224.

Moltmann, J. The Crucified God, London 1974.

Momigliano, A. 'Popular Religious Beliefs and the Late
      Roman Historians', Studies in Church History, eds.
      G.J. Cuming and D. Baker, vol. 8, 1972, pp. 1-18.

Moutsoulas, E. 'Der Begriff "Häresie" bei Epiphanius von
      Salamis', Studia Patristica VIII, TU 93, Berlin
      1966, pp. 86-107.

Nautin, P. 'Les fragments de Basilide sur la souffrance',
      Mélanges d'histoire des religions offerts à H.-C.
      Puech, Paris 1974, pp. 393-403.

——. Hippolyte et Josipe. Contribution à l'histoire de la
      littérature chrétienne du troisième siècle, Paris
      1947.

——. 'Histoire des dogmes et des sacrements chrétiens',
      Problèmes et méthodes d'histoire des religions,
      École pratique des Hautes Études, Section Sciences
      religieuses, Paris 1968, pp. 177-191.

——. Lettres et écrivains chrétiens des IIe et IIIe
      siècles, Paris 1961.

—. <u>Origène I. Sa vie et son oeuvre</u>, Paris 1977.

—. 'Saint Épiphane de Salamine', <u>DHGE</u> XV, Paris 1963, cols. 617-631.

Pagels, E.H. '"The Demiurge and His Archons" - A Gnostic View of the Bishop and Presbyters?', <u>HTR</u> 69, 1976, pp. 301-324.

Paulsen, H. 'Die Bedeutung des Montanismus für die Herausbildung des Kanons', <u>VC</u> 32, 1978, pp. 19-52.

Perkins, P. 'Irenaeus and the Gnostics. Rhetoric and Composition in Adversus Haereses Book One', <u>VC</u> 30, 1976, pp. 193-200.

Peterson, E. <u>Der Monotheismus als politisches Problem</u>, Leipzig 1935.

Powell, D. 'Tertullianists and Cataphrygians', <u>VC</u> 29, 1975, pp. 33-54.

Puech, H.-C. <u>En quête de la gnose</u>, 2 vols., Paris 1978.

Reynders, D.B. <u>Lexique comparé du texte grec et des versions latine, arménienne et syriaque de l'"Adversus haereses" de saint Irénée</u>, CSCO 141-142, Louvain 1954.

—. 'Optimisme et théocentrisme chez saint Irénée', <u>RTAM</u> 8, 1936, pp. 225-252.

—. 'La polémique de saint Irénée. Méthode et principes', <u>RTAM</u> 7, 1935, pp. 5-27.

Richard, M. 'Bibliographie de la controverse', <u>PO</u> 27, 1954, pp. 271-272.

——. 'Hippolyte de Rome', DS VII, Paris 1968, cols. 531-571.

Riggi, C. 'La figura di Epifanio nel IV secolo', Studia Patristica VIII, TU 93, Berlin 1966, pp. 86-107.

——. 'Il termine "hairesis" nell' accezione di Epifanio di Salamina (Panarion t. I; De Fide)', Salesianum 29, 1967, pp. 3-27.

——. Epifanio Contro Mani, Roma 1967.

Rudolph, K. Die Gnosis. Wesen und Geschichte einer spätantiken Religion, Göttingen 1977.

Sagnard, F.-M.-M. La gnose valentinienne et le témoignage de saint Irénée, Paris 1974.

Sanders, E.P., ed. Jewish and Christian Self-Definition, Vol. I: The Shaping of Christianity in the Second and Third Centuries, London 1980.

Schenke, H.-M. 'Die Relevanz der Kirchenväter für die Erschliessung der Nag-Hammadi Texte', Das Korpus der griechischen christlichen Schriftsteller. Historie, Gegenwart, Zukunft, eds. J. Irmscher and K. Treu, TU 120, Berlin 1977, pp. 209-218.

Schneemelcher, W. 'Epiphanius von Salamis', RAC 5, Stuttgart, 1960, pp. 909-927.

——. 'Notizen', ZKG 68, 1957, pp. 394-395.

Schoedel, W.R. 'Philosophy and Rhetoric in the Adversus Haereses of Irenaeus', VC 13, 1959, pp. 22-32.

Thouzellier, C. Catharisme et valdéisme au Languedoc, Paris 1969.

——. ed. <u>Le livre des deux principes</u>, SC 198, Paris 1973.

Tröger, K.W. 'The Attitude of the Gnostic Religion Toward
    Judaism as Viewed in a Variety of Perspectives',
    <u>Actes du Colloque international sur les textes de
    Nag Hammadi</u>, ed. B. Barc, Québec (forthcoming).

Ullmann, W. 'Gnostische und politische Häresie bei Celsus',
    <u>Theologische Versuche</u> II, eds. J. Rogge and G.
    Schille, Berlin 1970, pp. 153-185.

van Unnik, W.C. 'An Interesting Document of Second Century
    Theological Discussion', <u>VC</u> 31, 1977, pp. 196-228.

——. 'De la règle Μήτε προσθεῖναι μήτε ἀφελεῖν dans
    l'histoire du canon', <u>VC</u> 3, 1949, pp. 1-36.

Villain, M. 'Rufin d'Aquilée. La querelle autour
    d'Origène', <u>RechSR</u> 27, 1937, pp. 5-37.

Widmann, M. 'Irenäus und seine theologischen Väter', <u>ZTK</u>
    54, 1957, pp. 156-173.

Wisse, F. 'The Epistle of Jude in the History of
    Heresiology', <u>Essays on the Nag Hammadi Texts in
    Honour of Alexander Böhlig</u>, ed. M. Krause, Leiden
    1972, pp. 133-143.

——. 'The Nag Hammadi Library and the Heresiologists', <u>VC</u>
    25, 1971, pp. 205-223.

——. 'The 'Opponents' in the New Testament in the Light of
    the Nag Hammadi Writings', <u>Actes du Colloque
    international sur les textes de Nag Hammadi d'août
    1978</u>, ed. B. Barc, Québec (forthcoming).